MARTIN THORNTON

SPIRITUAL

DIRECTION

By the same Author:

Rural Synthesis
Pastoral Theology: a Reorientation
Christian Proficiency
Essays in Pastoral Reconstruction
Margery Kempe
The Purple Headed Mountain
English Spirituality
The Rock and the River
The Function of Theology
Prayer: a New Encounter
My God

SPIRITUAL DIRECTION

Published in Great Britain by SPCK.
Published in the United States of America by Cowley Publications.

Cover design by James Madden, SSJE.

International Standard Book No.: 0-936384-17-4

Library of Congress Catalog No.: 83-73658

Dedicated
with love and thanksgiving
to
Graham
Bishop of London

ROMANS 16.3a

Contents

Preface

IN MAY OF 1979 Bishop Graham Leonard asked me to initiate a substantial course of study for potential spiritual directors, both clerical and lay, men and women, in the hope that this would help to fill a notorious Anglican gap, and supply a growing need.

It did not sound too arduous a commission, yet the process of setting the course going, taking part in some thirty sessions, and entering into dialogue with others who are vocationally inclined to this ministry, has resulted in this book.

The first job was to create a syllabus, spread over four years, but suitably reduced for those already well grounded in biblical and systematic theology. That is a fair description of the present book: an extended syllabus covering the range of studies required for competent direction.

It then became necessary to think of the practicalities. Having absorbed the necessary knowledge, precisely how was it to be applied? What was the relationship involved? How do you actually begin to guide another in the progressive life of prayer?

Spiritual direction is a complicated business, a combination of art and science, with science as the predominant partner. It demands a special approach to a wide range of theological studies, and then extends still further, because Christian spirituality is no personal, hole-in-a-corner pietism but the source of love and the power of redemption. Eventually subsidiary disciplines like sociology, psychology and history play their part and finally, since Christian prayer is rooted in the Incarnation, cultural factors of particular societies have to be considered.

The perennial problem is that, while admitting the complexity of any interesting and worthwhile project, it all sounds horrifically worse when written down and printed. Write down all the knowledge required to drive a car from London to Manchester, then log every incident on the journey, every sign that must be read, every decision that has to be made, every minor misjudgement by oneself or by others, and there can be only one conclusion: to drive from London to Manchester is absolutely impossible.

I hope the book is not quite so bad as that. It is probably not since it comes as some surprise to me to be made to realize what I have been doing for the past thirty years. Were the book to fall into the hands of any of those under my spiritual direction I think they would be equally surprised to learn what has been happening to them.

Without more explanation or apology, the book arises out of our studies in Truro which are designed for those of some theological acumen, who feel vocationally called to this much needed form of pastoral ministry, and who are prepared to work at it seriously and continuously.

Chapter 1

Introduction: Bi-sociation and *Via Media*

SPIRITUAL DIRECTION is the application of theology to the life of prayer. Since prayer, as progressive relationship with God in Christ, is carried on in the world, it ultimately controls all aspects of life. It therefore extends into other disciplines and creative syntheses evolve: bi-sociation. Although prominent in the Anglican tradition as a whole, more particularly in the seventeenth century, spiritual direction has been notoriously neglected in the recent past, so it has to be both rediscovered and reinterpreted in contemporary terms.

There is, or should be, a parallel between spiritual theology and direction on the one hand, and biblical studies and preaching on the other. In courses of training for Christian ministry, the study of the Bible is followed and completed by consideration of the art and science of homiletics: how, in a particular age and culture, is acquired knowledge of the Gospel to be effectively proclaimed? Biblical studies find a corporate expression in liturgy, the practical know-how of which is taken at least as seriously as homiletics, but the ultimate value of liturgy depends upon the creative spirituality of each individual within the congregation. If serious study is given to preaching and liturgy, that is to the assembled community of faith, why is so little consideration given to personal development? There is still very little ascetical equivalent to homiletics or liturgical studies, which means that 'going to church' becomes an end in itself. Far from being a self-centred, inward-looking luxury, the development of individual spirituality is the true source of Christian influence and mission. But in the absence of any equivalent to homiletics or liturgical expertise, how is the spiritual direction of the faithful actually carried out? What is the knowledge required and how is it applied?

What follows is an attempt to answer these questions, first with

1

ference to the ancient and classical tradition, and secondly in an attempt to up-date this tradition in more contemporary terms, consonant with modern life, work and thought. Again there is an analogy with preaching and liturgy, which demand constant re-interpretation of time-honoured principles in tune with changing cultural patterns. But there is interaction between ancient and modern, and between theology and other disciplines. One cannot simply 'adapt'; more is involved than changes in vocabulary and idiom.

In *The Act of Creation*, Arthur Koestler introduces the notion of fortuitous bi-sociation, which means that creative ideas are apt to emerge when seemingly disparate disciplines are permitted to interact. It is akin to Hegelian dialectic, and points to the real meaning of Anglican *via media* in which the combination of two elements do not make a simple mixture but a new substance altogether. *Via media* has nothing to do with compromise; it is not concerned that red added to white equals pink but is rather analogous to the inter-action between oxygen and hydrogen which makes not a gaseous mixture but something altogether different. Anglican *via media* is no compromise between Catholicism and Protestantism but a bi-sociation creating a new spiritual ethos unique to Christendom.

From such a synthesis issues the Anglican principle of comprehensiveness, another term subject to misinterpretation. Comprehensiveness means that a wide diversity of Christian people, gloriously different in gifts and graces, outlook and temperament, can happily be embraced within a united ecclesial community. The principle gives high priority to personal spiritual direction, for it gladly recognizes unique individuality in everyone. In such a context, preaching to a congregation, group instruction, courses pre-supposing a common spirituality, can never be enough: deeply personal guidance is called for. It is no wonder that spiritual direction has played such a major part in the Anglican pastoral tradition. This tradition continues, but plain explanation of the practicalities involved is still largely lacking.

Comprehensiveness is prostituted when it is interpreted to mean that everyone has to be equal, the lowest common factor is the norm, nobody must be different, let alone better or worse, than anybody else. The error is perilously common to modern Christianity. But God dispenses his gifts with total generosity and alarming disproportion, yet always to the benefit of the whole. Traditionally the local church rejoiced in its gifted members and nurtured its saints; today serious attempts at sanctity are regarded as in rather bad taste.

A further bi-sociation is the seemingly unlikely marriage between ascetics and sociology. Recently my duties forced me to read a considerable amount of the latter discipline. As concerned with ordination training I thought I should know what nonsense higher authority had forced upon my students, so I set about the task with a conscientious lack of enthusiasm. In a vague way I had noted that there were still sociologists who made imposing graphs and much fuss about statistics relating to Easter communicants, infant baptisms and Church of England marriages, and I still wonder how on earth this kind of thing can be taken seriously, or how such figures can be made to mean anything. Less arrogantly I expected the better of the books to conclude with something not wholly insignificant about the Church's role in modern society and its influence, or lack of influence, upon its evils. I was humbled, surprised and put most happily in my place to find that some of these studies impinged deeply on the art and science of spiritual direction. Not only were new insights added to the directorial relationship and to the Church's liturgical function, but much of the orthodox ascetic tradition was substantiated and explained in a startlingly new way. My special thanks are due to the Reverend Bruce Reed whose *The Dynamic of Religion* forms the basis of Chapter 14.

Another insight, following contemporary interest in nineteenth-century studies, is concerned with the 'professionalization' of the clergy during the Victorian era (see for example, Ian Bradley, *The Call to Seriousness*; Brian Heeney, *A Different Kind of Gentleman*; Peter Hammond, *The Parson and the Victorian Parish*; Brenda Colloms, *Victorian Country Parsons*). The theme is clear enough. The eighteenth-century clergyman was a gentleman in Holy Orders, a disastrous idea but possibly less so in context than it appears at first sight: the word 'gentleman'—the only real qualification for the priesthood—has undergone substantial changes in meaning. But it was the age when dons and schoolmasters decided, or decided not, 'to take Holy Orders' rather in the spirit that one decides to take a holiday or to take a bath: a straight incidental choice without too much heartsearching

3

involved. A not dissimilar attitude pertained among doctors, lawyers, architects and schoolmasters: you did the job if you felt able and if you could convince others of your ability.

Throughout the reign of Queen Victoria, the professionalization process developed all round, which according to Anthony Russell (*The Clerical Profession*, p.13), was characterized by four dominant factors:

1. Professional practice was founded upon the basis of theoretical, esoteric knowledge.

2. This was learnt and inculcated through professional educational and social institutions: hence the rise of the residential theological colleges.

3. The inner ring of the profession exercised control over recruitment, training, dress and behaviour.

4. Each profession created and promulgated its own ethical system.

The Church followed the general pattern under the last three headings: theological colleges offered not only learning but also a distinctive 'clerical' pattern of life and outlook. It was no longer enough to be a 'gentleman'. The bishops began to exercise more control over selection and training of their candidates for ordination; M.A. Oxon was not in itself enough. Ecclesiastical bureaucracy arose and it continues unassuaged; no young man seeking Orders today is in doubt that there are professional rules, standards, attitudes and regulations to be considered. That there is an accepted social-professional-clerical ethic is still apparent—a pint in a pub in a dog-collar clearly proves the point—even if such an ethic is not quite so pronounced as in the more morally conscious Victorian age.

All of which is sociology of an interesting and pertinent kind, but it is the first point of Russell's professionalization process which needs further examination here. To the clergyman 'theoretical, esoteric knowledge' means theology, but precisely how was this to be applied to the needs of individual people? The other rising professions - law, medicine, architecture - offered no difficulty on this score, but the newly professional clergy struggled throughout the century to find an answer. Was it preaching? or liturgical expertise? or moral behaviour? None of these quite fitted the bill. It was not until the later Tractarian priest rediscovered spiritual direction that the social-professionalization reached its proper consummation. It is only in personal spiritual direction that priesthood-as-profession finally fulfils itself, as, to my humble astonishment, Bruce Reed's sociological studies make clear.

Our troubles were not quite over in the early years of the present century. As I have endeavoured to argue elsewhere, the Tractarians had the right idea but they chose the wrong model. Their spiritual guidance—at least from what we read—consisted of undigested snippets from the Counter-Reformation tradition, by-passing the supreme examples of the art presented by the seventeenth-century Anglican divines. We are now happily in a new era, returning to the real roots of that tradition, which grow out of the wider experience of Catholic orthodoxy.

At this point the sociologists offer another peripheral if illuminating insight. A recent survey began with the question: 'Do clergymen fulfil any useful function in contemporary society?' The overall answer—with a few dissentients—was 'No'. Was there any objective reason for this devastating viewpoint? Yes indeed, clergymen fulfil no social function because they do not do any work. But how do you know? Upon what assumption is this judgement based? Clergymen do no work because they are always at home. Is it not possible to do useful work, pastoral care, counselling, administration of the parish and so on, at home? No, not really. A few more dissentients admitted a grudging possibility that it might be possible to work at home in an amateurish sort of way, but real work meant going out to the office, factory, hospital or clinic.

A similar attitude applied to the medical profession in that the majority trusted the group practice, centralized in an efficient clinic, more than the lone practitioner with his surgery attached to his private house. The latter may be a wise and well qualified doctor but he was not taking his job seriously. The survey concluded with the statistical majority of housewives, more especially within the lower age-groups, preferring the supermarket to the friendly little corner shop, and this irrespective of price ranges.

This impinges upon our immediate concern. It carries us back to the nineteenth century when, despite theological college training, inner professional control and ethical ethos, the clergy were never quite sure what they were to profess: precisely how their theoretical esoteric knowledge was to be applied. Sociology helps to bring this problem up to date. The survey just described points to the same problem; the clergy are useless and out of work because they seem to have nothing very definite to profess; they stay at home.

Meanwhile ecclesiastical administration is being forced to move, halfheartedly and apologetically, into precisely those channels of which the populace approves. Group ministries embracing a number of small parishes, whether rural or urban, have to set up some kind of administrative centre: an ecclesiastical clinic with office hours and facilities for professional consultation. Modern cathedrals, without the dubious blessing of an aesthetically somnolent close, have to set up a complex of offices, meeting rooms, refectory and parlour, after the American pattern.

The Church looks upon all this as a necessary but retrograde movement, continuing to put its trust in the amateurish fireside-chat approach. Pastoral care is dispensed in the clergyman's home, spiritual direction is a woolly little waffle around the domestic hearth. At all events avoid the professional, and more especially the clinical. The point at issue is that in this book I am about to argue the opposite case; that not only is it clinical professionalism that we lack, and have lacked for a century and a half, but that it is precisely this that the Christian laity are demanding. Despite current nostalgia in the cathedral close, sociology insists that modern people have little use for the quaint old corner shoppe, or the dear old country doctor with his surgery tucked in amongst the shrubberies: they want supermarkets and clinics. My thesis is that they no longer have confidence in pastoral pietism over cucumber sandwiches on the rectory lawn. They want professionalism in spiritual direction: the application of 'theoretical, esoteric know-ledge'.

Backed by sociology, such is my case. But it is softened somewhat by further *via media*, bi-sociation. In the field of human relationships there has been a movement away from the analytic, the old faculty-psychology approach, towards synthesis. Human nature is to be respected *in toto*, personality is to be regarded as an integrated whole: people are people who are not to be treated as cases or cyphers or statistics. This is healthy enough, but social psychology, in its study of human relationships, points to an inter-relation between analysis and synthesis, rather than opposition of one by the other. This is the case that I will argue for the subtle relationship involved in spiritual direction. Following sociology in

6

rejecting the fireside-chat approach as a century and a half behind the times, I am to suggest that the most efficient, creative, and ultimately loving way to direct a brother-in-Christ is ruthlessly to split him up, classify and categorize him, according to the classical system of orthodox ascetics. Without apology I have headed chapter 5 'Love on the Slab'.

The final bi-sociation applies to theology itself, which follows this same pattern; from analysis to synthesis, or more technically, from the substantial to the existential. Any group meeting to discuss contemporary spirituality and spiritual direction will soon divide itself into a clear straight-down-the-middle split. On the one side will be a conservative element which swallows medieval orthodoxy uncritically and as it stands: Scaramelli can write no wrong. This approach will be opposed by a usually younger element who would scrap the tradition and start from scratch, because, it is argued, the Benedictine, Salesian and Carmelite traditions are all based upon a substantive, and therefore outmoded theology. As temperamentally drawn to the former group, I must nevertheless charge it with obscurantism and a certain lack of sympathy for contemporary people. The latter group have a stronger and more thoughtfully considered case; on the surface at any rate, some of the great spiritual classics must sound a little curious to computer engineers or political economists. But again why the conflict? Is synthesis, the true *via media* principle, a possibility?

I will argue that, from the viewpoint of spiritual direction, such a synthesis of old and new, substantive and existential, is not only possible but essential. If modern prayer is to be underpinned by a sound theological foundation, then that theology has to be expressed in contemporary idiom. Yet if the spiritual director is to attain to any competence he will be forced back upon the old substantive categories of the patristic and scholastic ages. Christology is an obvious case in point, which must be considered in detail later. Contemporary spirituality, following the current synthesis-versus-analysis approach, demands a modern christology stressing the risen and glorified Lord as integrated Person. It is concerned with an existential encounter with Jesus Christ in the world, and then with the experience of incorporation into the sacred humanity. It has no great interest in substantive metaphysics. Spiritual direction, recognizing this, is nevertheless forced back to the Chalcedonian categories, or something like them, as necessary analytical background. The old-school conservative is unhappy with contemporary theological interpretation; the modern radical rejects Chalcedon out of hand. It is only a synthesis of both that leads to competent direction.

Chapter 2

The Ambulance Syndrome

C. S. LEWIS said that if you aim for heaven you get earth thrown in, if you aim at earth you get nothing at all, which is but a succinct paraphrase of the dominical injunction: 'But rather seek ye the kingdom of God; and all these things shall be added unto you'. Jesus also said, 'I am come that they might have life, and that they might have it more abundantly.'

In the face of this most positive and purposeful heart of the Gospel it is curious that what we ambiguously call pastoral care is seen as something entirely negative. It invariably suggests the dispensation of human benevolence with a sprinkling of Christian saccharin: helping those in trouble, counselling the disturbed, solving human problems. This is the ambulance syndrome, implying that Christianity might alleviate suffering but that it has nothing more positive to offer. The pastor is there to pick up the pieces after an accident, and barring accidents he is out of a job.

The ambulance syndrome in no way denies the exercise of compassion in love and service for one's neighbour. All that is the background expression of Christian faith, but it is not the heart of the Gospel which is all about the kingdom of God initiated by the Resurrection and Ascension of the Incarnate Son and life more abundant in Christ.

Pastoral care is concerned with religion, with theology as its articulation. But here are two of the most prostituted words in current journalism; religion being reduced to cultic piety and theology as a synonym for ideological bigotry. Religion is about the living relation between man and God, God and the world, so ultimately everything comes under its purview. Theology is the clarification and codification of this relational experience, which rebounds as guide to its deepening development. This relation between man and God, given in baptism, continued by grace,

9

forged by prayer, is that life more abundant which Christ has promised. Prayer in its widest and deepest sense is response to this given status; it is an entry into the eternal realm, into the transcendent dimension, the kingdom of God, which through the Body of Christ is the one power of redemption for the universe and everything that is in it.

This positive development of the man-God relation, which is prayer; this application of the Gospel to human life, and not just to human need, is what pastoral care really means. And it is of the most ultimate social significance because it goes beyond problem solving, either individual or communal, towards redemption; it is not concerned with happiness but with joy, not with mediocrity but with glory.

Compassion, concern for the distressed, love of neighbour; these are both end-products of prayer and preparation for it. In technical language they are ascetic rather than moral qualities, adding redemptive depth to what is otherwise shallow humanism. Should we not look again at the meaning of pastoral care, seeing it again as the journey to heaven, not as a trip to hospital?

Here are some analogies which must soon be examined in detail. If you telephone for an appointment with the doctor I assume that his reaction, if any, is 'Oh dear what is the trouble with him'. The response of the golf professional in similar circumstances is 'Ah good, he wants to improve his game'. How would the Christian pastor respond? My regrettable hunch is according to the medical approach: now what can the trouble be? But Jesus did not offer life a little more bearable, he promised life more abundant; neither did he exhort his disciples to aim at a respectable mediocrity but to perfection.

Prayer—man's continuing relation with God—is neither a sop to make one feel better nor a pious interlude to solve problems: it is the peak of human achievement. Religion is no ally or appendage to philosophy or social science, still less a conventional bulwark to ethics and stability; it transcends all of these, piercing the visible and intellectual: it is life more abundant.

Spiritual direction is the way forward. It is the positive nurture of man's relation with God, the creative cultivation of *charismata*; the gifts and graces that all have received. It is the opposite of the sort of pastoral care which assumes that religion can only offer little bits of help in emergencies: the ambulance syndrome. And it is the obverse of what has come to be called pastoral counselling, or perhaps more fairly the necessary consummation of it; if counselling deals with problems, direction takes over as soon as they are solved.

It is necessary, therefore, to see spiritual direction as an autonomous technique, based on a specific body of knowledge. Cultural factors rightly impinge on prayer, but we need the courage to distinguish between genuine contemporary development and mere fashion, especially in theology. Let us attempt to explain the distinction by way of some examples.

In the 1930s 'mysticism' was all the rage; beginning with reputable academic studies of that absorbing branch of theology, it caught the popular imagination. But then as now there were very few mystics around, so people dabbled with it: it was the fashion, without cultural foundation or theological integrity. Latterly and by contrast, theology has been re-interpreted within the framework of existential philosophy, for the very correct reason that such philosophy is no artificial structure but an explanation and examination of how people have, for various cultural reasons, come to look on life. From this existential world-view, there has arisen a distaste for discursive, intellectual meditation, and a new quest for the simpler forms of contemplative prayer. Spiritual directors of a half-century ago would have done well to defy the fashion, for that is all that its mysticism was. Their modern counterparts will do well to encourage contemplation, because it is a genuine cultural development.

Another example is that the modern educationalist is forever pointing out that *educere* means to lead forth, or to draw out, a student's potentiality, as opposed to the old-style education that was content to stuff a head full of presumed facts. If there is any analogy with spiritual direction, then it is very up-to-date indeed, for this has always been its aim; to develop innate gifts and graces. But some educationalists, a significant minority, would go further and decry any and every attempt to teach a fact; true knowledge has to be self-discovered, it can only arise by trial and error, by personal experiment. To question this approach is to commit the most fashionable of all educational sins: paternalism. Within this context, the spiritual director can learn from the educationalist, but on the other hand he needs the courage to preserve his autonomy, and to insist that direction becomes impossible if certain theological facts are not plainly stated: even paternalistically! Indeed there is a wrong sort of paternalism, but it is difficult for someone to jettison the concept altogether when his traditional nickname is Father. Whatever the educationalists may say, direction occasionally requires that someone who knows something must tell it to someone who does not. We must not fear going against the fashion.

For whatever reason, by design or accident, or by fear of the unfashionable, clergymen are notorious for adopting the extreme, and in context the erroneous form of educational vogue. They exhort the faithful—quite paternally!—to their various religious duties: worship God, read the Bible, above all pray, but with never a paternal word as to how you actually do it. Prayer is something one is expected to find out about by trial-and-error experiment, but this will not do if only because pastoral experience shows that the errors are even worse than the trials. People want help, because prayer must be based on theology of a specialized and intricate kind, and but few of the faithful can reasonably be expected to find all that out for themselves. By all means draw out—*educere*—personal potential, individual gifts, but the very drawing out process demands the application of knowledge.

Finally, let us consider 'pastoral care' and spiritual direction in relation to the commonest area of pastoral concern: suffering, old age and death. All responsible people must be concerned with these perennial problems, politicians and sociologists no less than Christian pastors, but the latter are under constant pressure to conform to the secular and fashionable approach. This is wholly under the influence of humanistic hedonism: the ambulance syndrome, which only approaches suffering as something to be relieved. Spiritual direction might at least suggest the counter claim that it was rather something to be interpreted and creatively redeemed, which is a little more positive because neither side can get rid of it, and only religion comes up with the astonishing and unfashionable view that suffering is not the worst of all evils.

Modern society precludes the extended, four-generation family, so lonely old-age becomes a social problem, only relieved by death. Too often the Church panders to the secular fashion and joins in the benevolent hunt, offering comforts, compassion, relief, and generally picking up the pieces: the ambulance syndrome. But a few of the aged are Christians, endowed with the providential gifts of spiritual maturity and solitude, not to mention time on their hands: what a positive opportunity! Perhaps this is idealistic, and there are certainly pastoral difficulties, the greatest of which is that even the Christian aged have not received competent direction in the past to be capable of realizing their spiritual potential in the present. The simplest of all spiritual progressions is punctuated by the two stages when words give way to thought, and when thought gives way to prayer, so given proper background, the diminishing intellectual powers of the senile could be a spiritual advantage. Even given the proper background, direction in such a case would be difficult, but not impossible; it is not so different from the direction of that most neglected section of the Christian community: the uneducated yet highly endowed, in old-fashioned terms the peasant saint. Benevolence or religion? Are the devout senile bits of worn-out machinery to be kept oiled and clean or are they positive vehicles for spiritual power? And they have the tremendous advantage of preparing for death seriously; but again whose side are we on, whose fashion do we adopt? Is death the final tragedy or the ultimate victory, the greatest disaster or the final achievement? The answer is plain enough so long as we allow one proviso: Christianity is religion.

I hope this introduction is enough to give some clear idea as to what spiritual direction is all about, but let us conclude with some clear statements of fact.

1. Spiritual direction is concerned with religion, and intrinsically with nothing else. Religion is expressed in prayer, which is the ongoing relationship between men and women with God in Christ, inviolably given in baptism. Such prayer has to be worked out in the world; current cultural patterns are part of it, and ultimately it leads to practical action and service towards society at large. But only ultimately, and only if we stick to our religious guns and refuse to take the rest too seriously.

Spiritual direction assumes the centrality of prayer as power to act; it expresses the religious dimension rather than a diminishing cultural addendum to which respectable people nod assent without really believing in it. The practical out-going Christian is not someone who, vaguely inspired by Jesus, sets about solving the world's problems and trying to love his neighbour off his own bat—albeit autographed by Jesus. Rather he is one who, ontologically incorporated into the sacred humanity of Christ, becomes his redemptive instrument.

Not for the first time Aquinas got it right: prayer is 'loving God in act so that the divine life can communicate itself to us and through us to the world'. Christian action is not action of which Jesus approves but action that he performs through his incorporated, and therefore prayerful, disciples. If Christianity is anything, if it is to regain any earthly influence, it must boldly proclaim itself as religion.

2. It follows that prayer, developed through spiritual direction, is not egoistical. Christian prayer always involves a corporate element, with liturgical worship—common prayer—as its foundation and fulcrum. 'Private' piety, or even 'private' prayer, aimed at some sort of spiritual self-culture, is unchristian, heretical, and a contradiction in terms: there is no such thing. Yet spiritual direction is unashamedly individualistic, because it guides and develops that individuality without which corporate action and influence by the organic Church is impossible. A hundred flutes do not make an orchestra, and a hundred flutes all playing the same notes do not make a symphony.

We are again forced to cross swords with fashion, because fashion, insinuating itself into theology, confronts us with the idolatry of the group. The corporate element in prayer is vital, liturgy is central, but as an orchestra not as a hundred flutes all playing the same notes, and the principle of an orchestra is disciplined individualism. Doubtless there is a value in group-dynamic, as there is a liturgical dynamic, but ultimately a group cannot think any more than a congregation can worship; it is only the sum of their individual members that can be productive.

So direction implies a personal, one-to-one relation of unique subtlety and which, with the orchestra-liturgical analogy still in mind, prohibits rather than encourages unhealthy introspection.

3. Spiritual direction is the application of ascetical and moral theology to individual cases, enlightened by the tradition of the Church which includes contemporary insights. It is therefore objective, professional and in a sense even clinical.

14

It is objective in that its foundation in theology and experience provides for every type of unique individual, while remaining neutral to its own sub-divisions. It is neither introspective nor extrovert, neither worldly nor other-worldly, neither intellectual nor emotional, neither elementary nor advanced: it is any of these in accordance with the needs of the case in question.

4. It follows that direction ought to be, but generally is not, synonymous with 'pastoral care'. It is not something applicable only to those of 'advanced' *charismata*. Christian prayer is the total relation of a Christian with God-in-Christ, so its nurture applies to all the baptized.

Above all it is positive not negative, with little to do with helping those in trouble: that is ordinary Christian charity, not spiritual direction. It does not embrace the ambulance syndrome, picking up the pieces after the accident, except in so far as real prayer is, indirectly, the supreme help in trouble so long as we do not consider it as such but regard such help as a by-product. Prayer is also, indirectly, the best of all possible ways of loving our neighbour, but again only so long as we neither confuse the means with the end nor get them back to front.

Christianity is religion.

Chapter 3

The Guidance Game

THE HEADING to this chapter sounds a little light-hearted, but it is not intended to be facetious; it is meant to be biblical, for it derives from the central analogy for spiritual direction in 1 Corinthians 9.24-7, coupled with Acts 24.16, the training of the spiritual athlete: *autos asko* - I exercise myself, *askeo* - to train, *askesis* - ascetical. Athletes play games, and sometimes they play them very seriously. Athletes need trainers, coaches, guides and directors.

Here the word 'game' has another relevant connotation; it might help to counteract that grimness of idiom which characterizes so many of the classic textbooks. If prayer is the Christian's natural status, his everyday relation with God in Christ, no good purpose is served by pronouncing the word in a hushed plummy voice. Direction in prayer is a serious business, but it is an exciting thing as well, not the terrible ordeal sometimes implied.

There is another meaning: to be 'game', according to the Oxford Dictionary, means 'having the spirit of a gamecock; full of pluck, showing fight, spirited'—or 'to die game; to meet death resolutely'. That is the end-product of spiritual direction; if we can so guide others as to meet death resolutely, gamely, we have done our job well.

The heading, closely allied as it is with this central analogy between the spiritual director and the athletic trainer-coach, also suggests that as well as fundamental acquaintance with the game itself, practical techniques are also involved. The coach must know the game inside out, but he need not necessarily be an expert player himself.

I remain a little uneasy with too great a stress on what modern pastoralia calls 'ministerial skills'. Superficial technique is no substitute for pastoral theology, slick know-how cannot replace

The Guidance Game

genuine pastoral care with its roots in the gospel. Nevertheless ministerial skill has its necessary if subsidiary place in the total scheme of things; having absorbed the theory and acquired the tools, you still have to learn how to use them. However much we have forgotten of our initial training, clergymen of my generation —and perhaps later generations as well—recall the occasion when a battered doll was taken from the seminary cupboard so that we could learn how to hold a baby at the font. It is questionable whether such demonstrations deserve a place in a serious curriculum, they are certainly no substitute for the theology of Christian initiation, yet it is of some importance that, when the occasion arises, the newly ordained get the baby the right way round.

Let the question be put into concrete terms. Someone, rightly or wrongly, has the reputation for spiritual direction. A stranger requests such ministration and an initial meeting is arranged. What exactly happens? What is the precise relationship involved? How do you *do* it? The client—I shall soon explain my preference for this unideal term—is encouraged to talk about his prayer, his faith, his moral difficulties, and also, if the ambulance syndrome is to be avoided, about what he believes to be his particular vocation and especially about his potential gifts, graces, virtues and accomplishments. He would say something about his job, his home, his social and intellectual background—the cultural factor— and above all about his providential good fortune; about the problems and difficulties he has not got. The director listens, puts in an occasional question for some positive good reason, according to some background theological plan, but above all he listens; he is not there to discover social irrelevancies or even to take a benign interest in the chap generally. Then he is called upon to direct, to point the way ahead, to open up positive avenues of exciting experiment.

Is there any analogy here with the doctor making a diagnosis, a psychiatrist practising analysis, or a lawyer advising his client? Or of the coach training the athlete? In what sense is the consultation personal, professional, or clinical? How can the director *direct*? Or must the outcome be little more than friendly support, devout encouragement, and a few pious vagaries? Are we dealing with positive technicalities or do we settle for a cosy little chat? In other words who is, or can be, a spiritual director? And what are the skills and qualities demanded of him?

The classical tradition makes much of this, with each authority presenting a slightly different list of desired qualities, or roughly the same list in a different order: love, prudence, understanding, human concern and psychological insight, experience and discernment, all of which have some bearing on ministerial skill. But all authorities without exception top the list with *learning*. Knowledge of moral and ascetical theology and familiarity with the classical tradition, which is but a specialized application of the gospel, is always the prior requirement. Knowledge comes before anything, including personal holiness, because all men are different and personal sanctity can be, indeed must be, ascetically narrow. Saints can inspire but they need not be good practical guides for everyone. It is easy enough to direct someone whose gifts, graces and spiritual outlook are the same as one's own. The difficulty, and the skill, comes in the guidance of those whose spirituality is totally different from one's own; and nine out of ten of anyone's clientele will come into that category.

What too often happens is that an elderly and experienced priest acquires a just reputation for personal holiness; through many hours of prayer the light of Christ shines through him. Such sanctified men are wonderful to know, their influence on others is incalculable; the pastoral and evangelistic power of such a one could be miraculous. He surely, is a spiritual director; this must be the man to consult. But it is not necessarily so. That he has found, or been guided into, his own special way is no guarantee that he can guide others in their special way; and he could so easily fall into the disastrous error of trying to make all his clients pale replicas of himself, of moulding everyone in his own image which means pouring the majority into the wrong mould.

To be personal, I have much difficulty with intercession, and I have to fall back on very simple forms by way of duty. I get by because I believe that God can use such meagre offerings and that, in conjunction with the Eucharist, Christ can make up for my deficiencies. Others have a positive and pronounced intercessory *charisma* and it is my job to discern and encourage it as central to their spiritual lives. But I cannot do that without some under-standing of the theology of intercession, and without some acquaint-ance with the writings of the saintly intercessors of the past. I am not of the *via negativa* school; I can get on very well thank you without the *Mystical Theology* of the Pseudo-Dionysius, and I do not turn to the *Imitatio Christi* or William Law for my own spiritual satisfaction. But others need this approach, and I must study these books and try to understand their viewpoint if I am to be any use to such people. Learning comes first.

Spiritual direction was never a clerical preserve, neither was it traditionally reserved for the especially advanced or gifted. Cultural factors again impinge on the tradition, since a large proportion of classical writings are addressed to professed religious or to the pious nobility like Jeanne de Chantal. Not, however, because these comprised the gifted few but because of social factors dominating those ages: feudalism, illiteracy and serfdom precluded anyone else. Similarly, most of the authoritative books were written by bishops and priests, not because it is essentially clerical, but because nobody else could write. Yet there are significant exceptions in all ages, like Julian of Norwich and Margery Kempe in the fourteenth century, and a host of lay ascetical writers and directors in the seventeenth. But if lay direction is a minor yet perennial aspect of the whole tradition, it is especially prominent in Anglicanism and is now enjoying a healthy revival. This laicizing of direction and its wider application to anyone from ploughboys to stockbrokers is one of the happier signs of revival. (On the instigation of Bishop Graham Leonard, and with the continued support of Bishop Peter Mumford, the diocese of Truro provides a four-year course for potential spiritual directors, more than half of whom are of the laity.)

It necessitates, however, a good deal of adaptation from the classical tradition in accordance with the differing cultural patterns involved. The *Rule* of St Benedict contains fundamental wisdom from which we can still learn much; its stress on stability is relevant to any modern *askesis*, but a good deal of adaptation is required before it provides immediate guidance to the devotions of an airline pilot. Much acrimony surrounds the contemporary slackening of the traditional fast, yet it is sometimes forgotten that, by and large and with obvious exceptions, we live in one of the most abstemious ages in history. The Benedictine diet is a choice of two cooked dishes twice a day, one pound of bread and a pint of wine. I would happily settle for that, except that I could not manage all the bread. So if *askesis* means physical discipline in support of spiritual development, we have got to think again; there are many other things than food which are detrimental to the life of prayer, and which did not bother the Benedictines. Consumer economy, advertisements, television, package holidays, tobacco, gin, rapid transportation, and porn shops, impinged little on the spirit of Monte Cassino.

Or consider St François de Sales' advice to the girl at a ball: 'At the very time when you were at the ball many souls were burning in hell-fire for sins committed at dances or on account of dances. Many Religious and persons of devotion were at that very time in the presence of God, singing his praises and contemplating his beauty. Oh, how much more profitable was their time spent than yours . . .' Well yes, theologically examined the saint has here some sound points: habitual recollection, penitence, vicarious responsibility in prayer, perspective, and indeed, holy recreation. But confronted with an attractive, vivacious, and thoroughly devout young lady from Florida, I think I should have to put it rather differently.

In devotional and ascetical writing it is not only the idiom that changes with the cultural method; theology itself changes in form if not in content. The best of contemporary theology does not seek to alter the core of the eternal revelation, it seeks rather to reinterpret revealed truth so that it becomes more intelligible to the prevailing outlook. Professor John Macquarrie, for example, expresses the faith once delivered to the saints within an existential rather than a Platonic or Aristotelean framework, for the admirable reason that most modern people are existentialist in outlook, even if they do not know it. The claim, which in Macquarrie's case is wholly justified, is that nothing fundamental has been altered, only the expression, the framework, the setting. So contemporary theology can live happily side by side with patristic and scholastic modes of thought. You can use either and the result is the same, the one difference being that modern people usually get on better with the former.

Ascetical theology goes a long step further, because instead of accepting the old and the new as alternatives, parallels existing in a sort of theological *détente*, it marries them together into a creative synthesis. Simply put, the new helps towards theological understanding which can be put to devotional use, while the old categories remain the essential tools of the directorial trade.

Modern christology places the stress on the living Lord, the crucified, resurrected and ascended Christ in his glorified humanity;

the ever-present Jesus to be embraced, loved and adored, who is concerned with the world of men and women, the world of war and work, joy and tragedy. Older christologies were more concerned with the metaphysical attributes of the incarnate *logos*, with philosophical explanations of the God-man synthesis. But you cannot embrace, love and adore a theological formula; you cannot worship the Chalcedonian Definition, only the living Christ it purports to describe, and which modern theology presents more attractively. But—and here is the vital issue—in the spiritual director's tool bag, the attractive modern implement is found to be singularly blunt, while the old Chalcedonian categories remain invaluable, indispensable, and sharp. Contemporary christology introduces the living Lord, only Chalcedon can help the director to tell you what to do next.

In spite of all the exhortations in the Book of Common Prayer I doubt if anyone has ever managed to worship the 'Trinity'. I am sure that nobody could worship the doctrine of the Trinity; you can only worship God to whom the doctrine of the Trinity gives definition. St Augustine did his best so to define, while Macquarrie with the help of Heidegger makes the doctrine not only more acceptable to modern people but points the way to its contemplative use. Such contemplation of the Triune God is likely to need some guidance, and rummaging around in his tool-bag, the director will discover that the *De Trinitate*, assisted here and there by technicians like Origen, Tertullian, Athanasius and Aquinas, will supply the directorial implements that he cannot do without. The director is to direct not teach; his client does not have to be a theologian to become a saint. Sanctity, or even less ambitious development, does not demand familiarity with Plato, Aristotle, Heidegger, or even Macquarrie. Yet development is in jeopardy if the director is not a serious student of all of them. Professional knowledge is paramount. I hope that this whole aspect will become more apparent as the book unfolds.

I have called this chapter 'The Guidance Game', and I have attempted some apologia for it. Nevertheless, with reservations, I continue to speak of a 'spiritual director' rather than of a 'spiritual guide'. After much thought and etymological research I think that we must stick with 'director', although, like 'client', the word has its disadvantages. It smacks too much of post-Tridentine authoritarianism, of the wrong sort of paternalism, while I remain convinced that there is a right sort. 'Guide' rather than 'director' is typical of the Anglican tradition, yet the root meaning is much the same; not so much a tyrant, master or autocrat but one who points the way, who does not say take the first on the right, second on the left, under the bridge and veer right, but who says your direction is unquestionably NNE but there are several routes to experiment with and choose from. Unlike 'director', and in context, 'guide' still requires the adjective; we would have to write 'spiritual guide' all along, which would be clumsy and irritating. In contemporary idiom 'director' sounds a little like the company boss, but it is better than 'guide' which sounds rather like a tourist courier who might also be a boy scout's sister.

'Pastor' is too wide, 'confessor' too narrow, 'mentor' barely fits. The ancient Celtic 'soul-friend', recently made popular by Fr Kenneth Leech, is delightful, as is its Anglo-Saxon equivalent 'ghostly-father'. Not only is there a delight in these phrases, they are also as accurate as we can get, but they remain archaic, which is precisely what the present study is trying to avoid—St François de Sales and all that. I fear that we must stick with 'director', with the hope that allowance will be made for its shortcomings.

Without pedantry some discussion of key words is necessary and illuminating, because the director-client relationship is subtle and all important, while the terminology of ascetical theology, especially in the classic writings of saints, is notoriously ambiguous. If we have had a little trouble with 'director' we are now in for rather more with those he directs. But I think it is worth the effort, if only to explain the underlying significance of the relationship itself.

Chapter 4

The Relationship

TWO CURIOUS FACTS point to the subtlety of the directorial relationship. In the first place, while doctors have patients, schoolmasters have pupils, professors have students, and shop-keepers have customers, there is no single and simple word for someone who is being directed in prayer by another. 'Spiritual child' (or 'ghostly child' if you prefer the fourteenth century) is correct, but it suffers from the soul-friend, ghostly-father drawback as well as sounding a trifle sugary for the contemporary West. 'Penitent' is the usual term for one who practises sacramental confession, but like 'confessor' it is too narrow. The sacrament of penance may play a subsidiary part in spiritual direction, but it is not the same thing. One might venture into Anglo-French with 'directé' or 'protégé', but both are ugly and do not suit; the first is a clumsy invention while the second is either patronizing or, in common usage, only applicable to potential genius: an idea we are anxious to avoid.

If the director himself requires a degree of humility and not a little reticence, 'disciple' is out of the question. The classic tradition offers plenty of choice: beginner, penitent, neophyte, exercitant, catechumen, son, daughter, and so on, but none of these quite fits. Soul is the most popular, but it is prim, archaic and ambiguous.

That doyen of spiritual directors, Giovanni Scaramelli, employs a battery of words more or less indiscriminately, amongst which are *cliens* and *consultor*. Both words are usually translated client, and this makes the best of a difficult job. If the soul-spiritual-child group of words tend towards sentimentality, client suffers from sounding cold and clinical, but in modern context this is the lesser evil. It suggests a proper professionalism, the objective application of a body of knowledge to a personal situation. A further advantage is the hint that it is the client who seeks and initiates the relationship, and who must always make the first move towards it. Like other learned professions—which is what spiritual direction is—directors are forbidden to canvass for custom or otherwise advertise themselves.

What is good enough for Scaramelli will have to be good enough for us, and the master is not alone; tradition uses and softens the term, thereby helping to explain it in the religious context. The preface to the Douai Bible runs: 'They . . . [the saints] solicitous for us their dearest clients, incessantly intercede before Christ's Divine Majestie.' Paulo Segneri writes of 'the devout client of Mary, instructed in the Motives and Means of serving Her'. And our own Bishop Joseph Hall speaks of 'these flowers, true clients of the sun'.

The second curious fact underlying the subtlety of the directorial relationship is that, not only has the Church never managed to define it, but it has always employed no less than three inter-related analogies to explain it. Each one brings out important truths, yet each leads into distortion if not balanced by the other two.

1. The first of these is the *medical* analogy, associated with our Lord's power of healing, now conveyed to his mystical Body, and drawing upon devout legend from the example of Luke the beloved physician. The spiritual director is physician of the soul, one who heals, absolves, restores and maintains spiritual health, thus producing the conditions for growth. This analogy links the director with his function as confessor and moral guide, which, though a minor aspect of the total game, is not to be minimized. Whatever our *charismata*, our discipline, devotion and faith, sin is still the ultimate foe, the destroyer of prayer and the most serious obstacle to progress. This is apparent in our Lord's linking of sin with disease and healing with forgiveness: 'Go and sin no more, thy faith hath made thee whole.' To incite penitence, to absolve, and to arm his client in the fight against temptation, is central to the director's job. Yet religion is not moralism, and this analogy in itself is narrow and restrictive. Doctors can be positively concerned with health and hygiene as well as with illness, with birth as well as death, but by and large we tend to equate the doctor with one who cures disease, who only restores the *status quo*, and inevitably one

24

who picks up the pieces after an accident: the ambulance syndrome. This negative emphasis is the price paid for giving sacramental confession too large a place in spiritual direction, and, worse still, of confusing direction with counselling.

This first analogy offers further implications. It supports the tradition, the ongoing tradition that embraces both old and new, in that amongst all the qualities required in spiritual direction, knowledge has inviolate priority. Piety, virtue, experience, love, compassion, are valuable adjuncts, but any or all of these are insufficient in themselves: there is no substitute for ascetical theology. Integrity, loving care, bedside manner, human concern, personal charm, are all admirable qualities in a doctor, but they do not compensate for medical incompetence. Both medicine and ascetic, moreover, are developing sciences, founded on dogmatic facts—anatomy and the creeds; they are nevertheless consonant with new research and reinterpretation. Cultural factors also come into it; environment, upbringing, heredity, temperament, social structures and pressures, all have their place in both medicine and prayer.

In all professions, but especially in medicine, there is an acknowledged distinction between the general practitioner and the specialist-consultant. Spiritual direction follows the pattern; on the one hand there is the parish-priest/general-practitioner/ director, and the lay director of his fellow faithful; and on the other hand is the mystical theologian. From the pastoral viewpoint, the latter is the research expert, the final academic authority, and his studies are of importance to everyone. The former is the shop-floor man, the pastoral interpreter, concerned with the application of more generalized knowledge of first principles. The specialist is concerned with a narrow field of research to which he gives undivided attention, and this is his importance to the total picture. The general practitioner cannot get on without him—the most academic of theologians has his essential place in the pastoral sphere—yet it is the general-practitioner/spiritual-director who is better at the practical job. The heart expert might not be all that good at setting broken bones, and the preacher with an overall knowledge of New Testament theology should have more to offer than the specialist scholar who has spent the last ten years on the Epistle to Philemon.

The disastrous error is to assume an artificial dichotomy,

whereby scholars are deemed to have knowledge which is of no practical use, and directors are armed with ministerial skills unrelated to theology. The facts point to a working relation between the two; scholarship provides the raw material for developing ascetical theology, yet the processing of the raw material is not always easy, so the specialist retains his necessary place. The family doctor is right to acknowledge his limitations in the face of a difficult or unusual case. He is right to call in the specialist, and especially right to know which one to consult, but his professional integrity would be suspect if he packed patients off to hospital with sprained ankles and mild doses of influenza. The analogy supports the point that spiritual direction is not to be confined to the advanced or specially gifted. The general practitioner should be able to cope with serious cases but treating a child with stomach-ache is equally part of his job. The spiritual director should be able to discern the lower levels of mystical experience while offering serious guidance to the babes-in-Christ.

Enlightening as this first analogy is, it leans to the negative side, the ambulance syndrome, picking up the pieces, rather than looking toward positive progress. There will be distortion until it is supplemented by the others.

2. The second and central analogy derives from St Paul: 'and in this I *exercise* myself' (Acts 24.16), *askeo*, to train, exercise, endeavour, hence *askesis*—ascetic, ascetical. The key passage is 1 Corinthians, 9.24-7; the process of training the spiritual athlete. Here is the answer to the ambulance syndrome, all too prevalent in both spiritual direction and in the wider pastoral context. If the pastor is seen as one who helps in trouble, with nothing more positive to offer, the evangelistic task is tarred with the same brush; having rustled up a sizeable congregation the only remaining job is to keep things ticking over.

This is not to disparage either charitable service to the distressed or evangelism; it is to look beyond them and so to create the means for their attainment. 'So run that ye may attain' is St Paul's exhortation, or with the New English Bible's tougher punchline 'run to win'. We are too ready to settle for a draw before the game begins.

The *askesis* analogy points the positive way towards a purposeful development of the spiritual life in all of its richness, with the uncovering of special gifts, the encouragement of innate skills, the deepening of faith and love: life more abundant in Christ. A walloping great congregation is fine, and fun, but what most communities really need is a couple of saints. The tragedy is that they may well be there in embryo, waiting to be discovered, waiting for sound training, waiting to be emancipated from the cult of the mediocre.

So the director-client relationship moves from that between doctor and patient to that between coach and athlete, a mutual partnership aimed at a common purpose: *run to win*. We have had enough verbal gymnastics already but it is significant that the English language again lets us down, for there is no adequate word for an athlete being coached: player, pupil, learner, tyro, trainé, coaché, are all unsatisfactory. On the other hand, while sticking to 'director' in deference to tradition, 'spiritual coach' probably describes the director-client relation most accurately.

Coaching may involve teaching, but they are not the same; coaching is primarily a question of showing someone how to do something, with or without consideration of the theories involved. Coach and director need knowledge, but this can be either taught or practically applied, depending upon the various needs and abilities of the particular client. Neither is coaching the same as training, which by analogy, is more akin to applying the disciplines supportive of the Christian life of prayer; the narrower asceticism is contrasted with the wider ascetical direction. And coaching is hardly curing or healing although the eradication of faults—the forgiveness of sins—will have its initial place. There might even be broken bones which must be set and healed before the athlete can continue to develop his skills, but that is primarily the doctor's job although the coach will be concerned. The trouble with the ambulance syndrome is not that it mends the broken bones, which is an admirable thing to do, but that it stops when the healing is accomplished without going on with the positive game.

The doctor is properly paternal, the authoritative partner in the relationship to whom patients must be, to some extent, submissive. Coach and athlete form a mutual relationship, a partnership aimed at a common purpose: run to win. The coach, moreover, is not necessarily the better player—knowledge comes before virtue— and often enough the expert coach is not even a good player. (In my schooldays, Mr C. S. Marriott, the Kent and England spin bowler, proved to be a batting coach near to genius, while in no season did his batting average reach double figures. He knew the game, he knew the techniques, he knew exactly how each stroke ought to be made and inculcated how it could be made. That he could not do it himself made no difference.)

It is satisfying to play a game well but there can be greater satisfaction in coaching another to higher standards, vicariously rejoicing in his success. One of the supreme blessings for the spiritual director is to watch his client surpass him, which on the general-practitioner level frequently happens.

Subordinate to the coach–athlete notion, *askeo-askesis* also carries a military connotation; military rather than athletic training: soldiers of Christ preparing for battle. This analogy is popular within certain streams of tradition, and it plays a significant part within classic devotional writings, and not least in Christian hymnody. The emphasis is different, a little more authoritarianism, a little less joy, more penitential discipline and evangelistic fervour, but less contemplative stability. In terms of ascetical theology the two analogies come to much the same thing and should be considered under the same head.

3. These first two analogies complement and balance one another, but finally they must be placed within the context of a third, which broadly is the most fundamental of all. This is the *nuptial* analogy, holding a central place in Christian spirituality at least since the writing of the *Song of Songs*. The Christian life is expressed as a marital relation with God in Christ, hence the mystical marriage, the spiritual espousals, the bride of Christ, the celestial wedding-feast, the family of God, mother Church, and similar imagery. The significance of the analogy is inexhaustible; there is hardly a significant spiritual writer from St Paul onward who does not use it, and no spiritual director can fail to draw upon it.

Its doctrinal foundation is baptismal incorporation into the sacred humanity of Jesus, being and living 'in Christ'. Like husband and wife, Christ and man remain distinct entities while being ontologically and irrevocably joined: the twain are one flesh. The analogy may be pressed to the limit and its implications extended into practically every aspect of Christian living. But for present purposes its importance lies in the *domestic* emphasis and in the domestic relationship which finds its fullest expression in that between director and client. Priests are called 'Father' because of this analogy, their clients are called sons and daughters in Christ. 'Spiritual child' is still the most strictly accurate term for the director's client, although its rejection must be accepted for reasons already explained.

Perhaps we get as near to the truth as possible if we think of the old-fashioned family doctor, correctly professional and properly qualified but something of an old-established family friend as well. Perhaps the coach has served the same club, the same team, for a very long time, so that he has become something more than a paid functionary; one of the family in fact. The professional, clinical aspect of the relationship is essential and the doctor-coach notion supplies it, but here it can be softened by the element of domesticity.

To summarize, the director-client relation is a subtle one which can only be grasped by analogy or experienced in practice. It is an amalgam of doctor and patient, coach and athlete, father and son, brother and sister. The doctor cures, the coach develops talent, the father loves. The coach works for the good success of both athlete and team, the father for both son and extended family: heal, cure, love. The relation is intimate, because if prayer pervades the whole of life then every circumstance is, or might be, relevant. The doctor need not concern himself with his patient's politics, the lawyer need not bother with his client's morals, the professor has little interest in his student's finances. But the director needs, or might need, the total picture, not in order to be generally helpful, or to degenerate into a pastoral counsellor, or to solve personal problems, but because all aspects of life might impinge on the development of prayer.

In the last resort the relation defies analysis, it is unique, yet the classical analogies point the way.

Chapter 5

Love on the Slab

LET US START the process: the preliminaries are over and we are face to face with our client in the initial interview.

We are immediately confronted with another cultural implication, demanding further resistance to fashion. Contemporary thought is governed by the concept of synthesis; full commitment of the whole man, total being, authentic personality: so runs the jargon. One world against nationalism, one society without class distinction; there is much to be said for it.

Theology follows the pattern. Scholars no longer dissect the Scriptures verse by verse but look towards general themes; today's christological Jesus is a living and total Being without being analysed into attributes. If man is made in the image of God it is because, following St Augustine, they are both trinities in unity, but the stress is on unity. All of which has much to be said in its favour. The old faculty psychology is dead; psychiatrists treating the whole person as a whole person, and doctors recognizing a psychosomatic unity: ulcers can be treated by lessening stress as well as by cutting them out.

Spiritual direction, however, has to resort to analysis as well, both in theology and psychology. While recognizing the value of contemporary interpretation, it must also rely on patristic and scholastic categories.

In practice the client is to be viewed in this double light. On the one hand he is a beloved brother-in-Christ, a whole person in his own right, a complete human being beloved by God, of infinite value and dignity. There is our beloved brother, sitting in a chair and seeking our guidance, but this can only effectively be given by placing him—metaphorically speaking—on a stone cold slab, to be analysed, classified, sorted out and generally pulled to pieces. He is still to be loved, but to be effective our dear Christian brother has to become a client. It is all part of the game.

For the client should be led to see the relationship in the context of a game, albeit a serious one. A rugby player may send his best friend hurtling to the ground in a flying tackle, but nobody minds because it is part of the game, even if it would be criminal assault outside of that context. I move about in society treating my clients as friends, not as cases, conundrums, interesting phenomena, or ascetical types, any more than a doctor views his patients in terms of their symptoms. Yet if direction is to be competent and creative, love on the stone cold slab is absolutely necessary.

So we listen to our client talking as freely and intimately as possible. It is not always easy because, natural reticence apart, prayer, spiritual experience, gifts and sins, are notoriously difficult to explain or describe. We may have to put questions, prod and encourage a little, but they must be precisely the right questions and we must know, in theological terms, exactly what we are listening *for*. The only alternative is a cosy little chat which will not get anybody anywhere.

The process is a little like a botanist classifying a plant by means of his technical *Flora* directory. First he will examine the seed and find out whether it is a monocotyledon or a dicotyledon, the first and fundamental clear-cut distinction. Whichever one it is, it is not the other, so half the vegetable kingdom is eliminated. Then he might count the stamens, then the petals, then see how they are arranged, until eventually, by a long process of elimination, he will know what the plant *is*: species, genus, variety, strain. That is what we must find out about our client: species, genus, variety, strain.

It sounds clinical and cold-blooded, but it is all part of the game and our client is still dear old Thomas who will probably quite enjoy the game as soon as he knows the rules. It is the result that matters, for the botanist's knowledge can help the plant to grow and multiply: thirty, sixty, a hundredfold. There is no point in dosing up a row of peas with nitrogenous fertilizer, because peas are legumes that do not need it; but it is as well to know what a legume is in the first place. So it is inadvisable to offer affective gush and sugary piety to a Dominican because he probably does not need it and certainly will not like it. Subject a scrupulous conscience to a lot of little rules and you will do him injury; a modicum of mortification might bring a lax conscience to life. But first we must find out which is which: species, genus, variety, strain.

Now, at last, to brass tacks. What is the theological equivalent to monocotyledons and dicotyledons? What species and genera are involved? Where do we begin?

Baron von Hügel introduced an important term into ascetical theology (one wishes that he had done something about director and client). The word is *attrait* which means a person's natural spiritual propensity, his inclination towards or attraction to particular forms of prayer; hence the sort of prayer, spiritual outlook, or theological direction that comes most naturally to him. It indicates his species and genus, and so the kind of spiritual path he should follow because he is what he is. If *attrait* is a client's proper direction, it follows that this is the first thing for his director to discover, and such discovery may be achieved according to the botanist's *Flora* analogy; the process of eliminating everything the client is not until it is reasonably clear what he is.

Classical ascetical theology comes up with two fundamental, straight-down-the-middle divisions that give us our starting point. The first is:

1. *Speculative* and *Affective*

These are technical terms of some subtlety but they broadly distinguish the intellectual and the emotional; between formality and spontaneity, disciplined duty and self-giving love.

The speculative man need not be brilliantly clever, but he is interested in the intellectual side of things. He likes to know the reason why and benefits from such knowledge. According to his capacity, theology will play some overt part in his direction, but he must be protected against the theologian's fallacy of confusing faith in God with the acceptance of theories about God. Although the concept of duty will play a major rôle in his religious life he will rebel against paternalism, even the healthy sort. He will accept guidance, or he would not have sought it in the first place, but he will want to know the reasoning behind any course that is suggested.

He could be frightened of anything like 'enthusiasm' or more frightened still of 'superstition', his emotions are under strict control (perhaps too much so?). Religious experience, in any form, is best left alone. But he is disciplined and dutiful, perhaps morally legalistic, with conscience tightly bridled by moral philosophy, sound or otherwise.

The speculative's God is, predominantly, the transcendent Father, the Creator, majestic Being, tailing off into an almighty lawgiver or even a metaphysical Absolute. Jesus Christ is, again predominantly, the Divine Saviour-Revealer: just a bit more God than Man. The Holy Spirit is God all right, the Church says so, but he does not play too large a part in this man's prayer.

I am not for a moment suggesting that our client, however theologically informed, is going to talk like this. In the initial love-on-the-slab interview (or even confrontation which can be more creative than either mutual friendliness or paternal submission) this is the sort of way that his director is going to think of him: we are getting somewhere.

To the speculative man, prayer is reasonable and dutiful; corporate worship is central; the daily office acceptable, the Eucharist is more of a fact than a feeling. Atonement is a divine fiat, wrought by the Cross of Christ, penitence is genuine, but do not expect many tears. He would express with Fortunatus: 'Sing my tongue the glorious battle . . .' and might feel a little uneasy with: 'O'erwhelm'd in depths of woe . . .' He might manage the meditations of St Bridget of Sweden but not the Little Flower of Lisieux.

Our speculative client looks a pretty odd fish, but all fish look a little peculiar on the cold slab. Allowing for obvious over-simplification for purposes of explanation, and not forgetting that this is the first major division with plenty of sub-divisions to come, his attitude finds strong support from every Christian century, from St Paul to St Thomas Aquinas, and then from a great body of Anglican divines: true piety and sound learning, or in less conventional language, don't let your heart run away with your head.

The affective man is roughly the opposite. He is quite properly emotional, and if he is Anglican-Saxon probably a little ashamed of it. He should be convinced that he need not be. He might or might not be capable of understanding theology, but in either case he will not be interested. He may feel guilty about this too, and again he need not be. The speculative and the affective are confronted with straight alternatives: the former hesitates to follow direction without knowing the reason why, so he will think and read and argue until given direction makes sense to him; the affective client need not bother with all this cerebration on condition that he does what he is told, which he is usually happy enough to do. But he will enjoy the affective saints: St Bernard, St Francis, George Herbert.

His *attrait* is likely to be towards the sacred humanity of Jesus, who is above all the suffering and loving Redeemer. The indwelling Spirit, especially in his role of Comforter, inspirer, sanctifier, will also play a major part in affective prayer, while the transcendent element could be under-played. Formal, run-of-the-mill prayer directed in praise of the Father—the divine office—could be something of a necessary burden; let that be fully and frankly admitted.

To the speculative man the Eucharist is the expression of a divine fiat and a means of grace; to his affective brother it is primarily a communion with his Saviour. They are both right and they are both courting distortion through imbalance.

Confusion may arise in that some strands of traditional ascetic regard affective prayer as a progressive step up from vocal prayer. That may be true in so far as affective prayer is something that one can develop and grow into, but it is also a gift, or state or *attrait* with which some are naturally endowed. Many, on the other hand, may by-pass affective prayer altogether and advance beyond it, and in some degree both may co-exist. Any such discussion as this cannot avoid over-simplification; there are blurred edges and overlaps all along the line, yet the distinction is sufficiently vivid to form a safe guideline of immense value. Despite the clinical approach it is never forgotten that the client on the slab is also beloved Thomas, a complete and unique human being. So the botanical analogy breaks down if pushed too far; a legume is a legume is a legume, two seed peas of the same variety and strain can be relied on to behave in much the same way and we can be quite certain that they will not produce beans. Humans are not quite so consistent, pronouncedly speculative people can have or acquire affective qualities, nothing is clear-cut, and if every human being is a unique creation there are infinite computations relating to his spiritual make-up. There are always exceptions to the rules of ascetical analysis, and it is juggling with the exceptions that constitutes the skill of the game. Nevertheless the clinical, love-on-the-slab analysis provides the necessary clues, the outline map of the spiritual country and a reliable compass. The only alternative is a cosy little chat.

2. *World affirmation* (kataphatic) and *World renunciation* (apophatic)

This second broad division is not quite the same as worldliness and other-worldliness, or as extroversion and introversion, still less with laxity and discipline. But there is something of a parallel with the ancient moral distinction between humanism and rigorism. The key to the difference is spiritual response to creation. World affirmation means not so much that the world is respected and enjoyed but that prayer is linked to the senses and focused on material objects, which may become vehicles for religious experience and intuition. St Mary Magdalene is the archetype; the true contemplative whose mystical insight was expressed through material things: crumpled graveclothes, boxes of perfume, her human tears and hair. St Francis of Assisi comes into the same class, with his devotion to God revolving round sun, moon, water, birds, animals and insects; yet he certainly was not 'worldly'.

The twin doctrinal foundation of this outlook is the doctrine of creation and of incarnation, with a strong stress on the sacred humanity, especially as it expands into theories of the cosmic Christ, the recapitulation of all things in the incarnate Lord as expounded by St Irenaeus. World affirmation involves a deep love for creation which is more than aesthetic, indeed it need have little to do with the beauty of nature. Creation is seen rather as the scene of divine activity, a proper arena for Christian life to be carried out; creatures, whether roses or rubbish makes little difference, can be vehicles for divine disclosure, as was a net full of squirming fish to St Peter.

Those in this category may manifest a healthy, Chestertonian zest for the good things of life, for all is shared with the sacred humanity, but it is not worldliness in the pejorative sense. On the other hand they could be sternly disciplined and austere, like St Francis, because of their reverence for life. The heart of this approach is a wide sacramentalism, with a full-blooded acceptance of the human body and its senses: grace perfects nature. Indeed the bodily senses can lead us astray, there is always the problem of sin, of lust, gluttony, covetousness and sloth, but the approach is by way of redemption not suppression. The prayer of affirmation begins, not with kneeling down and closing one's eyes, but with standing up and opening them as wide as possible.

World renunciation gropes after the mystical, the relation between man and God unmediated by anything else; material creatures are not evil, they are a nuisance that get in the way. It is the *via negativa*, issuing mainly from the writings of the Pseudo-Dionysius around A.D. 500. The movement is easily misunderstood, especially when presented in negative terms: the cloud of unknowing, the dark night, rich nought, dazzling darkness, and so on. But this sort of thing can provide very positive theology. Suffice it to say that the renunciative, *via negativa*, approach is an *attrait*, pointing in a positive direction to those who are made that way. Their inclinations are unpopular, and a little off-putting, but the director's job is to discern this *attrait* when he meets it and to guide accordingly. It is probably obvious by now that I am on the affirmative side, but confronted by the opposite, perhaps the lonely little bachelor with mystical-Quaker-leanings, it is my job to honour his *attrait*, and help him to develop the gifts God has given him, and to resist the inclination to make him more like me: God forbid.

But, without realizing it, how many of the sanctified old-style directors, without learning but with some terrible substitute called sanctified common sense, do just that?

Here arises another cultural dilemma, for *via negativa* spirituality is unpopular with both the ethos of the Western world and with reputable modern theology. We have no use for following the fashion, but in this case the fashion has a good deal to commend it. The world-affirmer is likely to be a little bashful in face of the tradition; to feel slightly ashamed of himself, a little inferior and second rate: should he not ride more lightly on the material side of things and take mortification a bit more seriously? On the other hand, the world-renouncer can easily become arrogant, and if not sinfully vain then just a little too pleased with himself. Both should be assured that we are dealing with types not qualities, there is no question of right or wrong, better or best. The director's job is to ascertain *attrait*, to decide on which side of the fence the client actually is.

Nevertheless, although we would decry the contemporary fashion of exaggerated immanence, a far too heavy stress on earth rather than heaven, on Christ in the market place to the detriment of the majesty of the Father, it is difficult to square *via negativa* mysticism with incarnational theology. The ultimate danger, which is unquestionable heresy, is angelism, the quest for pure spirit by the suppression of the bodily senses; dissatisfaction with the human state and a veiled desire to be as the angels. Crudely put the argument runs that if God does not eat and I do not eat then I become more like God, which is the sin of Satan who was dissatisfied with his created status: *the* original sin.

Sin itself, however, demands serious mortification, and world-renunciation holds too strong a place in the Church's tradition to be lightly discounted.

Two principles follow this analysis. First, we are still dealing with both dear Thomas and a client on the slab. If, for the sake of argument, there are a hundred types of spiritual *attrait*, we have now reduced Thomas to one in twenty-five: he is speculative so he is not affective; he is affirming so we need not bother him with Dionysian mysticism. By the time we have examined him under the light of all the clauses of the creed we will have a pretty clear idea of what he is—species-genus-variety-strain. Despite Thomas's unique humanity, his wonderful refusal to conform too neatly, despite the essential blurred edges of the analysis, the director has firm footholds.

The second principle is that we are concerned with *attrait*, which is to be respected and encouraged. Simple, uneducated, and not very intelligent people can be saints; the historical tradition is full of them, and it is both useless and needless to bother them with theology. No good purpose is served by offering sugary devotion to the strongly speculative. Nevertheless the ideal is perfect balance: true piety and sound learning, and the fourteenth-century English School has probably come closest to this ideal. Julian of Norwich is almost impossible to classify, being both deeply emotional and intuitive, yet intensely theological at the same time. One thinks of St Thomas Aquinas as the outstanding speculative genius, yet he wrote some deeply moving hymns. Similarly, affirmation and renunciation reach something of a synthesis in Eastern Orthodox spirituality, especially in its Russian strands. This strain is controlled by *via negativa* mysticism, yet it is profoundly influenced by the doctrine of creation.

There will always be some distortion; *attrait* is to be generally encouraged yet occasionally disciplined. Like pruning roses, cut in order to encourage, but do not try to mould a vigorous rambler into a compact bush.

Chapter 6

The Categories: Ancient and Modern

THE TRADITIONAL CLASSIFICATIONS just discussed are of great antiquity. They are firmly rooted in theology, and are of universal application. Living prayer, however, has to be carried on in the world, which means not just any world but the one with which one's client has to cope. We are back with the cultural factors, with the application of ancient principles to modern needs. So it is necessary to look for distinctions, down-the-line classifications— species-genus-variety-strain—which are peculiar to the contemporary situation, and which will be treated in the classical textbooks either obliquely, demanding considerable reinterpretation, or not at all.

While combing the textbooks for hints and clues I am here forced back on my own experience, which is very shaky ground indeed; nevertheless the following distinctions seem to have arisen fairly recently, and no harm will follow noting them.

1. 'Amateur' and 'Professional'

As always, the distinction refers to type and not to quality; yet it is pertinent that, returning to our *askesis*-athletic analogy, an amateur may well be a better player than a professional. The significant point is that, irrespective of intrinsic ability they approach the game in a different way.

Bishops and priests, monks and nuns, are professional religious, the former because they get paid for it and the latter because they are 'professed'. The tradition leans heavily towards this side, the bulk of orthodox ascetical theology having monastic roots or a pronounced clerical colour, and although we may applaud the increasing strength of lay-direction and lay theology, it is likely to remain minor to the clerical side of things for quite some time.

Outside Holy Order and monastic order, the professional-type

Christian has been around for a long time, in the form of tertiary, oblate, or recognizable holy matron. He or she is likely to need, or at least favour, all of the traditional ecclesiastical and devotional trappings: pictures, images, icons, texts on the wall and some sort of distinguishing badge on her person, cross or crucifix as a necklace, and a nunnish sort of veil in church. Here is the client who will talk freely about the faith, about her prayer, knowing the jargon and adopting it with enthusiasm. All of which helps the director a great deal.

This professional client will have a contemplative love for her parish church and the paraphernalia it houses; not just a keen parishioner, still less an admirer of ancient architecture, but happy in a prayerful environment. He could be something of a medievalist, again not through a shallow romanticism but by *attrait*, revelling in elaborate liturgy, and being especially drawn to the Reserved Sacrament.

The professional client, whatever the underlying *attrait*, will incline towards the conservative position, the conventional (in both senses!) attitude, and he or she will take the minutiae of ecclesiastical etiquette very seriously, kissing the episcopal ring with abandon.

The 'amateur', like the proconsul Gallio, cares for none of these things: or not much. He is the man who is no less prayerful, no less faithful, no less disciplined, than his professional brother but whose spiritual life takes a different line. He is probably, if not necessarily, speculative and affirming; so the omnipresence of God, his incorporation into Christ, are such obvious facts that there is little to make a fuss about. Habitual recollection, albeit based on formal prayer, is the keynote of his life; Christ is present in history and event, the divine providence a fact of life. He is not anti-social, playing his proper part in parochial affairs, but he does not want to join societies, third-orders, or groups—especially prayer-groups. He will support the vicar at the parish Eucharist while secretly preferring low Mass on Monday morning.

His life is hid with Christ in God, with stress on the hid. His amateur sister is much the same, but perhaps with a greater domestic emphasis in the sense of Anglican-Benedictine 'homeliness'. Habitual recollection is still the keynote, because that is what 'homeliness' means; contemplative focus on material objects, some created thing, is important to her, but a scrubbing brush is as good as a crucifix. There will be no icons in the kitchen because what is wrong with a cabbage? There will be no oratory-like corner in her house because a flop in an armchair is as good a prayer posture as kneeling at a *prie-dieu*. She might make an occasional retreat, but she will not spend her life on the convent doorstep. She wants direction but she does not want to be organized, and if she has a day in the country with her brother the very last thing they will do is visit country churches.

There are golfers who must kit themselves out according to the fashion, not that they are vain but that they have to feel the part before they can play well. There are others of equal skill to whom any old clothes will do for a game of golf. The former will get a tremendous kick out of playing at St Andrews; the latter is perfectly happy on his home, third-rate links.

This distribution can be dug out of the ascetical tradition: the ecclesiastical St Peter of Cluny, with everything correctly magnificent, and St Francis in his rags, wandering around anywhere. St Teresa of Avila, Mother-Superior *par excellence*, and Margery Kempe, who could never have joined any sort of society, let alone been the head of it. Yet I think that in the present cultural situation the distinction takes on new facets, which are of importance to direction.

With the present over-emphasis on the group, the conference and the club, individualists get a raw deal. Direction is essentially a one-to-one relation, and ought to be a loner's bastion. But enthusiasm can pressurize the wrong sort into oblation and tertiary fraternities; professional groups quite unsuited to gifted amateurs. Directors who are parish priests are prone to this error; parishes are blessed when they have a traditional association with an established religious order, with an oblate core of common rule and purpose; but would it not be wonderful if everyone joined in? Well perhaps, but not at the expense of amateur *attrait*.

The point raises the difficulty and delicacy of the relation between the spiritual director and parish priest. In rare cases these might be one and the same person, but such would be rare because it is inviolable to Christian tradition that all, even including professed religious, have absolute right to choose their own director. In any case difficulties remain. It is unlikely that anyone under serious guidance will be parochially disloyal; he is precisely the one who wishes to assist the priest in creating harmony and progress, and any director of competence will assist him so to do. Yet *attrait* must be respected; the amateur, who has links with the solitary of tradition, must be allowed to develop his gifts for the good of all and not be dragooned into groups and movements which could stunt that development.

The Sunday sung Eucharist is the high point in the parish week, and certain sacrifices of one's own inclination form part of the game, but nobody need be surprised or shocked if the amateurs prefer Monday mornings. How important that our parish churches are used, prayed in, daily and continuously, and all honour to the parish priest who gives this top priority, yet amateurs under direction, with so much to give to the total parochial organism, are generally happier at home: if prayer is habitual recollection of and in the sacred humanity, why should you need a special place for it? Another sacrificial curb is suggested, but the amateur attitude deserves respect.

This is a modern distinction, even if hints of it are found in the past. The Cistercians embraced both choir monks and *conversi*, whose oratory was the open field. The Franciscans rebelled against over-elaborate liturgy. The English or German anchoress achieved the mystical heights without vows, rules, badges or distinctive dress. The *Devotio Moderna* movement tended towards the amateur as well as being lay and secular. It is possibly a correct emphasis on the theology of the secular, currently in the fashion, that gives this distinction its topical importance.

2. *Grim* and *Gay*

Throughout Christian history there have been dour ascetics (in the narrow and popular sense) and troubadours of God: the *Imitatio Christi* and St Francis of Assisi. To the writer of the Shepherd of Hermas, cheerfulness is the essential ingredient of Christian prayer; to many of his successors prayer is grim, dour, difficult and dutiful. In the hymns of Venantius Fortunatus, the Cross of Christ is the most glorious of victories; to the majority of late Victorian hymn-writers, it is the greatest of tragedies. The golden era of Anglican spirituality came up with John Cosin and William Law, but also with John Donne and Thomas Traherne. More recently our Roman brothers have produced Cardinal Ottaviani and John Henry Newman as well as G. K. Chesterton and Ronald Knox. Orthodox theology will not take sides because we are back to *attrait* rather than rights and wrongs. So the distinction is important for direction. Is the Cross victory or tragedy (speculative versus affective)? Does Christian life centre on the Crucifixion or the Incarnation (renunciation or affirmation)? Is the Gospel Good News or Good News with ominous undertones? Apart from the medieval liturgist's peculiar system of priorities, where is the living down-to-earth focus: Christmas, Good Friday, or Easter Day? Theology still has no firm opinion to offer, except to say that any of these attitudes constitute reputable *attrait*, that we are involved with paradox, and that, because of sin, there is bound to be a modicum of distortion all along the line.

Throughout the ages, ascetical theology has taken note of psychological distinctions; early in Christian history, Galen produced his classification which included the melancholic and sanguine temperaments, which, long after Freud, continue to be taken seriously if in different terminology: eschewing the jargon, and in the context of direction, grim and gay answer well enough.

Spiritual guidance is a serious business, or rather a game taken seriously. On the whole, and despite the foregoing historical introduction, its literature is awesomely grim, everything is desperately tense. These ancient distinctions become culturally topical when it is seen that there is a special modernity about the art of seriously taking serious things as lightheartedly as possible: 'sick humour' is an illustration.

The contemporary dilemma is that, accepting the distinction that some clients like seriousness and some like gaiety—the suggestion of a half-time glass of sherry will send some scuttling off and greatly relieve others—spiritual direction is generally regarded as mainly grim while hymnody is Fortunatus revived: 'Sing my tongue the glorious battle . . .' or

> *I danced in the morning when the world was begun,*
> *And I danced in the moon and the stars and the sun,*
> *And I came down from heaven and I danced on the earth—*
> *At Bethlehem I had my birth.*
>> *Dance, then, wherever you may be,*
>> *I am the Lord of the Dance, said he,*
>> *And I'll lead you all, wherever you may be,*
>> *And I'll lead you all in the dance, said he.*

In spite of this cultural movement within the Church itself—
from stiffly regimented rows to dances around the altar—modern
spiritual direction remains Good Friday centred. This criticism is
not for a moment to play down the importance of the perennial
fight against sin, which is the most positive fight there is, but we
need an ascetic of the incarnation and resurrection to balance
things. Positive life in the resurrected Christ is more than morality,
and prayer which sustains it not wholly confined to the penitential
emphasis.

This shows up the error of equating direction with the
sacrament of penance, or even of giving that glorious means of
grace too large a place in it. Although the situation would not be
ideal, Anglicans have to accept the possibility of serious direction
without recourse to sacramental confession at all.

The upshot is that, although the grim and the gay—Newman
and Chesterton—are both valid approaches and are both to be
found in contemporary religion, the general stress is very much on
the grim. Direction is seen to be something difficult and tense.

If a client finds himself in some painful situation, direction
might, for example, revolve around the concept of divine
providence. It could be expressed, with Fr Raymond Raynes, by the
supposition that God is God and he is quite impossibly awkward,
or with Lady Helen Oppenheimer that God has little propensity for
playing fair. Even St Teresa complained that God treated his best
friends badly. That sort of idiom expresses the doctrine of
providence very well, but only those clients of gay *attrait* could
take it, or even see the point. Others could be deeply shocked,
so the same doctrine would have to be expressed in another
way.

I once served in a group of Norfolk villages, two of which were
called Gayton (Gay Town) and Grimston (Grim Town) and they
were aptly named. Villages take on corporate personalities and
these two perfectly illustrate the point. Gayton had a cricket team,
a football club, a school, three pubs and plenty of social life;
Grimston had nothing very much. I could preach a sermon at
Gayton, illustrate it with little jokes and everyone would roar with
laughter; the same sermon at Grimston would be met with the
stoniest of silences. Gayton understood both the awkwardness of
God and the good humour of Jesus; I do not think Grimston did.
(Perhaps I should add that I loved Grimston dearly, that I am

talking of thirty-five years ago, and that no doubt things have changed.)

On the whole the literature of spiritual direction is well weighted on the grim side; it is so very serious and heavy that many are put off the whole business. If we are concerned with God's gifts, graces, life more abundant, then this is silly and out of character. But *attrait* comes first; a minority of clients prefer the heavily serious approach, and they are entitled to have it. The director's job is to discover which approach suits the particular client best, and try to follow it, irrespective of his own preference.

The principle of both encouragement and balance still applies. The lighthearted can be sanctified lightheartedly, yet a gentle tug of the reins towards the other side may be necessary. The seriously solemn also need encouragement to go their own way, but solemnity might turn to scrupulosity and it might preclude joy. The distinction remains a useful one.

3. Class distinction

How unfashionable can we get! There is neither bond nor free, Jew nor Greek, male nor female: all are one in Christ Jesus. The other side of the paradox is that human beings are unique creations and there are no two alike. Talk of class distinction today is about the most unfashionable thing there is, and many will wonder what on earth it has to do with spiritual direction and with prayer. But whether we like it or not, cultural factors creep in, and they vary from age to age.

St Louis IX wore a hair shirt under the royal ermine, and St Francis gave away his inheritance in order to embrace brother louse under his sackcloth; which points a moral but it all sounds a little unreal. Is there a parallel between a modern Christian merchant banker and St Louis, or between the frugal family man who happens to own an oilfield and St Francis?

The classic tradition offers little help to what is a genuine distinction in direction. Right up to the middle of the nineteenth century, pastoral ascetic was directed either to the burdened poor or to the leisured aristocracy, and there was not much in between. Today the issue is less clear-cut; the categories interact, creating a whole new range of social strata, which are cultural factors impinging on prayer. While recognizing personal *attrait* the

45

classical tradition has much to offer Sardinian peasant women (affective-world renouncing—they have not much choice) or Italian nobility (speculative-world affirming, because their culture proposes theology as the in-thing and it is difficult to run a large estate on the principle that God's creation is of no importance). But although fundamental ascetical principles remain valid, this traditional teaching is of little immediate relevance to bright young executives, graduate housewives, and air hostesses.

Whether or not the Church of England continues to be a middle-class affair is a moot point, but, however unpopular, class distinction subtly pervades its pastoral thinking. We set up industrial missions, aimed at the workers on the shop floor, and hope that the board of directors will co-operate; but there is no mission to the board of directors. We all know the story of the country squire congratulating the vicar on a sermon about sacramental confession: 'Excellent, Padré, just what *they* want.'

We have missions to seamen, missions to prisoners, missions to youth, and missions to the Jews, but why is there no mission to stockbrokers? Pastoral guidance is offered to children and to the aged, to the sick and to the distressed, while it is tacitly assumed that the churchwarden bank manager can look after himself.

Now whether we like it or not, all this concerns spiritual direction. The approach to the company director and to the woman who cleans his office is different, not because they are unequal in the sight of God, but because they themselves will approach direction differently; responsible authority and financial dependence produce different pastoral theological viewpoints. At one time I was concerned with the guidance of a little remnant in a small village, and it included a country girl who could only sign her name with difficulty, but whose intercessory gift was little short of miraculous; a retired schoolmistress, and the local master of foxhounds. All are indeed one in Christ Jesus, but these three serious Christians simply did not approach spiritual direction from the same angle. The sacrament of penance is impersonal and objective, but again the approach here was different, from the joy of the girl to the terror of the MFH. Not perhaps a deeply pastoral insight but there are times when a nice cup of tea assists the interview and there are other times when a large Scotch is a not invalid aid to the directorial process.

The point can be summarized in a story. A group of perspicacious priests in a certain English diocese were worried. They had good, as well as large, congregations. Their parishes were alive in the deeper sense, with plenty of daily communicants, directorial clients and the rest, but something was wrong. There was some subtle impediment, some diabolical influence, which precluded creative witness. A consultation was arranged between pastoral theologians, sociologists, and various other experts. The unanimous conclusion was that prayer was stunted, worship dulled, and witness ineffectual, because the whole Christian area had a guilt complex about being wealthy. It is different with Holy Trinity, Wall Street, or with St Mark's, Philadelphia, either of which could buy up that English diocese lock, stock, and barrel. My impression is that those parishes serve the cause of Christ wonderfully well: they are very rich, they take direction seriously, to share their worship on Good Friday is a penitential privilege, and there is no guilt.

The story may be reduced to a personal level. Men of distinction face cultural pressures against taking prayer seriously, and the same guilt-complex takes over. St Francis was the real saint, but is not there something phoney about Louis IX? No one doubts the sanctity of the Little Flower of Lisieux, but was not Madame de Chantal something of a religious dilettante? Squires and stockbrokers make wonderful churchwardens, but could God possibly have endowed them with *charismata*? In direction such cultural pressures have to be taken into account; approaches differ as they must have done for the spiritual directors of St Francis and St Louis.

Here are but three minor directorial distinctions of special topicality, to which the textbooks refer only obliquely. There must be others to be discovered and examined. Ascetical theology, like any other sort, must move into new interpretations according to changing cultural patterns.

Chapter 7

The Ascetical Syllabus

ASCETICAL THEOLOGY is that body of knowledge which is necessary to the spiritual director; the deep and intricate mine from which the tools of his trade are quarried, or which provides the raw material from which they can be made. Ascetical theology is vague and vast—vaguer still when it is called spiritual theology, and ambiguous when it is reduced to 'spirituality'. Take up a book with any of these words on its title-page and one is never quite sure what to expect. This enormous range is understandable once we see that we are dealing, not with another subject but with an approach to all theology; with its living embodiment, its practical end-product: prayer.

This wide range of knowledge necessary for competent direction is thus rendered a little less forbidding when it is realized that a good grounding in general theology is the prior requirement, and anyone with such a grounding has gone quite a long way along the road. It is its practical application with which we are to be concerned. We are back to the relation between homiletics and biblical studies; there is an art of direction as there is an art of preaching—to use the dictionary definition of homiletics—and if preaching assumes a knowledge of the Bible, so direction assumes a knowledge of ascetic.

Nevertheless there are areas which, from a practical point of view, need to be discussed. In the first place, and in view of the vast vagueness of the subject, it is necessary to see clearly what it is and how it is made up. Then we must see how it can be applied today, which means more up-dating of the traditional material. We need an overall syllabus, a framework against which the director's continuing studies can be fitted. Such an outline syllabus is made up of four inter-related departments (see also Appendix I).

48

(A) *Bible and creed*

The basis of all Christian prayer is the Bible, to which is added the historic creeds and the great doctrinal formulae seen as the Church's interpretation and distillation of it.

(B) *Ascetical theology proper*

From this foundation derives a secondary strata which is more usually, and more narrowly, called ascetical theology. This concerns the quest for perfection involving the sacraments, the development of the cardinal and theological virtues, the gifts of the spirit, the discernment of spirits or the interpretation of religious experience; the divisions, types, methods, and *regula* of prayer, spiritual progress and so on.

It will treat of the fight against sin, especially with regard to those physical and mental disciplines which are both weapons for this combat and supportive training for prayer: 'asceticism' in its narrow, popular, and inaccurate sense.

This second stratum thus combines the necessary negative with the ultimate positive: it is concerned with picking up the pieces after a sinful accident, with massaging away the bruises and mending the broken limbs, but only in order that the spiritual athlete can get back into the game.

(C) *Moral theology*

From the same foundation—Bible and creed—running parallel with the previous heading yet tightly intertwined with it, is moral theology. This will consist in the divisions of grace and human response to its action; sin, also in terms of its types and divisions, the varieties of conscience with its training and development; casuistry or the art of moral decision-making; the doctrine of man, his purpose and his end, with analyses of human temperament, *attrait*, psychological make-up and the impingement of cultural factors upon it.

(D) *The schools of prayer*

Now, and only now, comes that vast mass of teaching which issues out of the experience, experiment, and organization of the saints and doctors of the Church throughout the ages; the inexhaustible range of monastic order, the multifarious schools of prayer, the personal nuance of the great directors: everything that is popularly lumped under the heading of devotional literature or spiritual reading.

Together these four areas constitute the barest outline. The inter-relation of (B) and (C) is obvious enough, as should be their mutual foundation in (A). The edges overlap, and yet, unfashionable as it may be, the distinctions and analyses are of value; inter-relation without analysis invariably leads to confusion. The fourth area (D) is the glorious diversity of Christian expression all of which is nevertheless the end-product of (A) percolating down the ages through (B) and (C).

Such a system is required if the student, and the most venerable of directors remains a student, is to keep his vision clear. It is a popular error to regard section (D) as the core of ascetical theology, detached or detachable from Bible and creed. It is assumed that the saints, especially those on the affective side of the fence, prayed according to some intuitive hunch without reference to the doctrinal facts behind the revelation. Then proceeds the disastrous notion that you can become a competent director by lapping up the devotional literature without bothering with theology.

In truth, the glorious diversity of the saints and their respective schools derives from their juggling with the clauses of the creeds, stressing one great fact of revelation, arranging the others all round it in a new pattern, and leaving nothing out. So St Benedict looked at doctrine and saw that the Blessed Trinity could be practically manifested in the three-fold *Rule*: hence Benedictinism. St Bernard saw that a key to Christian life could be in sharing human experience with the sacred humanity of Jesus: hence the Cistercian school. St Francis saw God in creation, in birds and rivers and flowers, which precluded personal ownership: hence the much misunderstood ideal of holy poverty and Franciscanism. St François de Sales looked at creation too, but from the opposite direction; had not the secular élite any place in the redemptive scheme? Could not king and courtier be true disciples without abdication for monastic order? They could: so the Salesian school arose. It goes on for ever, but whatever the emphasis and whatever the diversity, it always starts with Bible and creed.

Conversely, while those steeped in the classical devotional writings without much biblical or theological background feel themselves competent directors, there are those who know their systematic theology very well yet disclaim all knowledge of ascetics, meaning the devotional writings of the saints: the senior wrangler who finds difficulty in adding up his change at the supermarket. In fact, the latter group are much nearer to competence as directors than the former. All these need is an exercise in adaptation and application. What the former need is a five-year course in biblical, patristic, and scholastic studies. Given an ideal setting, the popular preacher can enthral his congregation with all the latest existential developments in Christian thought; another popular preacher can trot out the old dogmatic clichés and, again given the suitable situation, reap applause. The spiritual director has to know both.

It boils down to a thorough grounding in (A) which, through application, leads into (B) and (C) which in turn is expressed and consummated by (D). That is the syllabus, which in one sense is unashamedly academic; even the most exciting writings of the saints have to be studied for their theological content as well as for their inspiration, if the director is to be of any use to the majority of his clients whose *attrait* will be different from his own.

Despite this necessary learning, however, little will be achieved without the director's personal spiritual struggle, disciplined and unceasing. The coach needs experience, especially of the struggling sort, and the best coach is frequently found to be the one who has tried and failed over and over again. The objective study of (D) is necessary, but it is to be supplemented by treating the same material as 'devotional reading', that is as basis for experiment in prayer itself. For the director, and not for his client, much can be gained in experience and technique by occasionally using books which he finds uncongenial. Struggle rather than brilliance is the surer foundation.

Because of the cultural factors involved in living prayer, the foundation study of (A) has to include contemporary theology. It is time to spell out in more detail the ancient-modern interplay. It is frequently held by the younger and more liberal theologian that the classical systems, which still uphold the Book of Common Prayer for example, have somehow slipped their theological moorings, that biblical and doctrinal studies have outstripped ascetical studies; that general theology has moved into the twentieth century while prayer and worship remain stuck in the Middle Ages.

Such criticism has much to justify it, for despite all the talk about 'contemporary spirituality' there seems to be precious little of it about. This is not to say that there is little prayer about, but that it becomes of the experimental hit-or-miss variety with little theology to support it. Those modernists who wish to sweep away the whole classical tradition must face the fact that those temperamentally attracted to that tradition are the happy ones, for they have a theological foundation of proven efficacy. Nevertheless, those clients who are repulsed by the tradition should be respected, served and guided with sympathy. Confronted with such clients there is not much to go on, and what we have, however original and up-to-date it may sound, is invariably traceable to some saint in the past.

There is much to be done in the formulation of a contemporary ascetic, but with reference to both ancient and modern theology. There needs to be synthesis rather than opposition.

The nub of the matter is the distinction and interaction between the synthetic and existential on the one hand and the analytic and substantive on the other. Patristic and scholastic theology is of the latter kind, treating, for example, of the 'attributes' of God: what is God like? Contemporary reinterpretation is of the former sort, claiming to speak in terms of experience and function: how is God experienced and how does he act?

It is something akin to the difference between giving a reference and making an introduction. The first comprises an analysis, a list of attributes or qualities: John Smith is conscientious, honest, hardworking, reliable and so on. The second runs differently: dear John, your whole integrated person, I should like to introduce Mary, all of her, as she is.

In the directorial relationship, on the cold slab, both approaches have their place. It is important to discover John's attributes—affective, affirming, amateur, Franciscan—and he will get on better at prayer if he realizes something of the attributes of God, omnipotence, omnipresence, transcendence, immanence and so on. But the end-product of all this is an introduction, or the furtherance of a relationship, between John and God, Mary and

Jesus. By the normal rules of etiquette an introduction can only be made by one intimately acquainted with both parties.

The knowledge summarized under this composite ascetical syllabus—(A), (B), (C), (D)—gives the director creative *entrée* into the heart and mind of his client. He is placed in a most intimate relation with an affective, world-affirming, immanentalist, with a conscience inclined to laxity, Cistercian *attrait*, Nestorian leanings, and a slight Trinitarian imbalance towards the Third Person.

It sounds a curious description of the total, integrated, existential Thomas, beloved child of God, beloved spiritual son; who, being a reasonably intelligent twentieth-century solicitor, will make more sense of Professor Macquarrie and Dr Hans Küng than he might of St Augustine and St Thomas Aquinas.

The vital thing is that we are speaking of one and the same chap.

Chapter 8

The Bible

THE BIBLE is the source of all Christian doctrine, and it is this doctrine, the creeds and dogmatic formulae, which are of more immediate use in spiritual direction. There is no opposition, since doctrine is the distillation of the biblical revelation, and therefore its articulation into usable formularies. The Bible itself comes into its own as the vehicle for meditative and contemplative use, as the basis of prayer, while doctrine is the tool with the sharper cutting-edge for direction itself.

Nevertheless, the Bible could be the source of ascetical theology as well as of doctrine; of practical teaching about prayer as well as its inspiration. But here the criticism of the modern radical seems to be more than justified, for with few exceptions, such as Archbishop Coggan's *The Prayers of the New Testament*, and Professor Jeremias' *The Prayers of Jesus*, few modern biblical scholars seem concerned with this aspect of the revelation. Perhaps the practice of prayer has slipped its doctrinal moorings, at least in this germinal field. The larger ascetical studies of recent date, like Louis Bouyer's *A History of Christian Spirituality*, are mostly disappointing. This criticism could be unfair in so far as this work is called a *History*, which is what it is, but as such it offers little to the spiritual director.

There is much to be done in what appears to be a most fertile Ph.D. field. We have New Testament ethics, New Testament liturgy, New Testament ecclesiology, New Testament christology, but you have to look a long way for New Testament ascetic. And the Old Testament fares worse, so badly in fact that it is more or less written off as of any devotional value; there are studies on the sacrificial system, on synagogue liturgy, and on the Psalter, but again they are approached in a way that gives little encouragement to spiritual direction.

Claiming no special expertise in biblical studies, I can only point to certain biblical bases of orthodox patterns, in the hope that they might be considered worthy of further consideration by those better qualified.

It is sometimes argued that ascetical theology is an artificial and superfluous subject, invented by professional religious and maintained by academicians with nothing better to do. There is one simple gospel, the argument goes, and one simple response to God in prayer: why all the fuss? Why the cold slab? This argument can be dismissed by three briefly stated facts. *First*, the gospel is not all that simple. *Secondly*, everyone is different—thank God—and any real relationship has a uniqueness about it. Fundamental principles are involved, and these apply to everyone, but once you ask precisely what these are you are immersed in theology, and therefore in ascetical theology. *Thirdly*, a simple relationship with Jesus in prayer is marvellously possible for the saints, but most of us have not got quite that far: so sin plays merry hell with the simplicity. Sin makes for complication: ascetical theology becomes important.

From the point of view of the client, especially if he is of the affective type, such criticism of ascetical theology might seem to be justified. Categories, patterns, analyses, plans and divisions, seem remote from actual praying, but we must keep our eye on the ball, and if all this is admitted, ascetical theology remains the essential tool-bag for the spiritual director. How he uses the tools therein contained is for him to decide, that is the skill of the thing, and whether or to what extent he bothers his client with ascetical theory depends on the specific needs and *attrait* of the client in question. But the director himself must know this theology, and he must also be assured of its biblical and doctrinal validity. The following very brief synopsis may help to underpin such validity.

1. *The Regula*

The Benedictine *regula*; the trinitarian pattern of divine office, Eucharist, and personal devotion, has held sway within orthodox spirituality for fourteen centuries. It has been subjected to criticism for almost as long, and it has been constantly modified, expanded, reinterpreted and changed in detail. Today, with

particular reference to the divine office which forms its characteristic core, it is the prime Aunt Sally for radical opposition, while
those in its favour have to admit to certain theological im-
perfections in the system. Be that as it may, the point in question is
that it is not a monastic, *sui generis* invention of St Benedict, but is
of biblical derivation.

Matthew 6.9–13 and Luke 11.2–4, give dominical authority to a
set form of words which is to be 'common' prayer: the *Pater Noster*
is the original office, and it still fulfils its common purpose in so far
as it is impossible to imagine any Christian church, denomination
or sect that does not use it. On the other hand, Matthew 6.6 points
to personal, uniquely individual prayer, and this is supported
throughout the New Testament. In the present context, we can
take it for granted that Christ instituted the Eucharist.

The root of the thing goes further back, as has been pointed out
often enough. Synagogue worship, especially in its use of the
Psalter, the Jewish sacrificial system, and Hebrew prayer in general
all point ultimately to the Christian–Benedictine transformation.
Professor Jeremias' *The Prayers of Jesus* substantiate all this with
startling clarity. The *regula* is no monastic artificiality but a
biblical system.

2. *The Three-Ways Progression*

The classical teaching that Christians progress, or ought to
progress, from purgation of sin, to illumination by grace, and
finally to union with God, is also subjected to much criticism, and
not least through misunderstanding. The misunderstanding is
perhaps excusable since much of this teaching is presented with
considerable ambiguity. Modern critical opinion regards the
scheme as, at worst, an artificial construction which is also
meaningless or even dangerous, or at best as an oversimplication
of observed fact but without theological foundation.

Whatever the shortcomings of the system, however, it can make
a fair claim to biblical foundation. If prayer is in essence
relationship between man and God, it is first expressed in the Old
Testament in terms of *covenant*: a bond or contract whereby God
pledges support in return for obedience to given laws, social,
liturgical and moral. It links with the purgative way in several
respects: both contain a strong ethical element, God is remote—

'out there'—either through our sin or his transcendence, yet the covenant pledge assures his intervention in worldly events. He is a useful God, an ambulance syndrome God, who helps in trouble. That may be a little unfair to the Hebrew patriarchs and prophets, but it is a good enough pastoral description for beginners—those in the purgative way—and it gives more than a clue as to how they are likely to behave and how they should be guided.

The second biblical stage leads up to, and is consummated by, the incarnation. Here covenant gives way to *encounter*, or illumination, since God is more clearly manifested in his revelation in Christ. In the prayer of encounter or the illuminative way, God is closer, more intimate, the relationship of prayer is richer since it involves colloquy, conversation, question and answer, and therefore personal leading rather than impersonal obedience to objective command. Grace replaces law; inspiration, illumination, personal discipleship, loyalty, all play a bigger part. So the prayer common to this stage is vocal and intellectual on the speculative side; and meditative, with strong stress upon affective imagination on the affective side.

Thirdly and finally, comes the great Pauline conception of *incorporation*. By baptism the Christian is 'in-Christ', incorporated into the sacred humanity, sharing the resurrected and ascended life in Christ. And this, literally, is union, with some form of contemplative absorption as the norm of prayer.

The trouble with the three-ways scheme is that it is extremely complicated to interpret and apply, and unduly easy to misapply. But it has a biblical foundation which is pastorally conducive to further exposition (chapter 12).

3. Moral theology

Biblical ethics, more especially New Testament ethics, is no new thing, yet that specific moral theology which bears more directly upon spiritual direction is sometimes assumed to be divorced from it. At first sight, the minute distinctions, divisions and subdivisions of sin in scholastic theology may appear to be unreal, artificial, or even plain silly. The Thomist doctrine of grace is even more intricate and complex. But the point is lost when it is understood that none of this is meant to be, primarily, factual explanation or straight theology: it is rather the manufacture of delicate tools to be put into the hands of a skilled director. Much ascetical and moral theology is like an old-type open razor; admirable in the hands of a skilled barber but best not left lying around for any child to play with. K. E. Kirk's oft-quoted comment on the mortal-venial sin distinction sums the thing up very well and is worth repeating: 'From the point of view of God, so to say, it is unreal; from the point of view of the sinner himself, it is dangerous. There is, however, the third point of view: that of the priest whose business it is to try to repair the damages caused by sin to human souls. And from this point of view the distinction between mortal and venial sin is both real and valuable.' (*Some Principles of Moral Theology*, p. 247)

But even this curious distinction is traceable to the New Testament (1 John 5.16-17), and so is most of the rest, however much adaptation and expansion it has received later. In the same way, the Decalogue ends up as the more sophisticated list of capital sins *via* the ethical teaching of Jesus. The moral progression follows the pattern of the spiritual progression just discussed—covenant, encounter, incorporation, underpinning the three ways—since the cardinal virtues are very much of an Old Testament flavour. These are then supplemented by the theological virtues of 1 Corinthians 13, and consummated by the gifts of the Spirit in both testaments: Isaiah 11.2-3; Galatians 5.22-3; and finally as a spiritual progression in 2 Peter 1.5-7.

Old Testament, or covenant prayer, is ascetically important because it is of a type that never wholly disappears from any Christian life, however advanced it may be, and also because it is the first stage in which many people are, and, regrettably, in which they are apt to get stuck through lack of competent guidance.

4. *The Old Testament prayers*

It follows that directors would benefit from an ascetical study of the great prayers of the patriarchs and prophets. Directors benefit from making such a meditative study themselves but they would be even more assisted if Old Testament scholars took up the work as well: another significant Ph.D.

It is argued that the Old Testament God is not the Christian God, but then a good deal of the prayer of Christians is not

Christian prayer either. Covenant relation is a necessary starting point, as is the Hebrew conception of God; an enormous amount is lost by sliding over, or even blatantly omitting, the bloodier, cursing bits of these great prayers, especially in the Psalter. The fierce, angry, terrifying, even vindictive God, is a necessary step in the spiritual pilgrimage towards the Christian conception. Undirected and unfought for, for the impenitent beginner, the God of Love can be a misleading idea.

The Psalter is the obvious starting point, for it introduces the widest range of prayer in its initial stages; from liturgy to the intensely personal, from pure praise to the most intimate petition, from God the transcendent Father to God the fairly crude personal helper, and from the God of Love to the despotic terror. There is distortion when anything is left out, which is one reason why it is the most quoted section of Scripture by our Lord himself, and why it is unlikely, despite radical objection, that a substitute will ever be found. To construct an office without psalms is practically impossible, and to replace psalmody by hymns or contemporary religious poems is to throw out ascetical theology, and therefore spiritual progress.

The book of Job has already received attention as an example of the long, hard pilgrimage towards human conformity with the will of God. The creativity of suffering as redemptive agency, the mysterious workings of Providence—even God's awkwardness and unfairness—is here plain to see. The subtler aspects of the nuptial analogy, with its origin in the Song of Songs (which mature Christians should pray very seriously) is also evident.

On the surface, and here very much on the surface, the great prayers of Moses offer pointers towards the ascetical riches therein enshrined. Exodus 32.11-14 and 33.12-23 is superb colloquy, inspired by the honour of God and the need of the moment: in Christian terms of trinitarian balance. The second prayer is also full of such insight as well as teaching of wider pastoral concern, concluding with the hidden God, anticipating Christian contemplation of a sophisticated, *via negativa* kind. Numbers 11.11-25 is that sort of creative colloquy which arises out of a bold argument with God, very much the prayer of the sanctified and receptive spiritual mind. Deuteronomy 9.18-21 and 25-9 are jewels of penitential prayer.

Abraham's intercession for the city of Sodom (Genesis 18.23-32)

Spiritual Direction

sounds curious, even funny, yet it suggests a stage-by-stage
spiritual exercise that St Ignatius Loyola might have constructed,
while its pastoral implications, interpreted ascetically, are such as
might make many a modern parish priest think very hard indeed
about his pastoral strategy.

Here are but a few tentative examples of the kind of studies in
spirituality that might be possible by those qualified to pursue
them. May we optimistically look forward to such titles as *The
Contemplative Technique of Deutero-Isaiah*, or *The Ascetical
Theology of Lamentations*? The immediate point is that if firm
foundations are of any consequence, the Old Testament is source
not only of spiritual inspiration but also of sharp new tools for the
spiritual director.

5. Biblical typology

There is nothing particularly new in this form of biblical
interpretation since it was employed by St Paul and was allowed
somewhat to run riot by the school of Alexandria. Its ascetical
content has been undervalued, yet here is a rich source for spiritual
direction. A few examples must again suffice to introduce its
possibilities.

Dr E. L. Mascall has drawn out some inspiring and thoroughly
practical teaching on the concept of *rest* as contemplative
consummation of activity (*Grace and Glory*). From the Genesis
creation stories to the Epistle to the Hebrews the type persists:
God's sabbath rest is the ultimate creative act, his contemplation
in love for the universe which remains its source of being; while the
rest promised to the people of God (Hebrews 3.11, 18; 4.1ff.) is
their active contemplation of the vision of God, the consummation
of all earthly activity. The practical value of this teaching to the
secular, world-affirming client—the so-called 'mixed life'—is
enormous.

I have myself attempted a typological interpretation of the
desert or *wilderness* in conjunction with the prayer of, and
practical use of, silence (*Prayer: a New Encounter*, pp.168-70).
Summarized in 1 Kings 19.4-18, contemplative silence begins
with turmoil, danger, fear, discomfort, which gradually turns into
peace, security and calm; from psychological alienation ('concupiscence') to psychological integration ('contemplation'), with

60

the possible end-product of prophetic inspiration. But there is more in it than that, and much remains to be done.

The *cloud*, which plays its part in Exodus 33, previously discussed, is the type for God's hidden immanence, from the cloud from out of which he spoke to Moses and led the Exodus, to the cloud of the Ascension narrative. The image is germinal to *via negativa* mysticism and central to its negative terminology: *The Cloud of Unknowing*. Once more its ascetical theological importance is incalculable.

The *garden*, from Eden onwards, provides almost complete analogical illumination for the spiritual life. It is fenced—by the Church, by *regula*, by God himself, against the devil, danger, and sin. There is grace-fertilization, pruning-mortification, seed sowing-germination-fruitfulness, allied with death-rebirth-resurrection-glory. There is winter and summer—aridity and consolation; there is peaceful contemplation and penitential labour, the rooting out of the sinful weeds and the gentle tillage of affective prayer. It goes on for ever!

This analogy contains the type of *water*, with its connotation with baptismal washing, purifying, and refreshment. *Marriage* is central through the nuptial analogy, the *banquet* plays a large part in most speculations about heaven, and there is *light* and *darkness*, the *mountain* and the *plain*, the *rock*, the *pit*, and many more.

6. *The New Testament prayers*

The move from the Old Testament to the Gospels is the move from covenant prayer to the prayer of encounter: incarnate in Christ, God is closer, more approachable, and less terrifying. The great prayers of our Lord himself—John 17 and Gethsemane (which has close associations with the desert-wilderness typology)—are obviously inexhaustible in their meaning and depth, and they have been studied often enough. But if prayer is encounter, then any relation between Christ and people, depicted in the Gospel narrative, is consonant with ascetical, as well as ethical or doctrinal, interpretation. The encounter between Jesus and the disciples, between Jesus and Zacchaeus, or the adulteress, or the woman at the well, or St Mary Magdalene, are all prayers, and may be examined as such.

The Samaritan woman (John 4.7-26) is ascetically parallel with aspects of Moses' prayer in Numbers 11.11-25. There is bold argument with God leading to a prophetic conclusion, but in the Gospel the tone is softer. Moses, despite the colloquy-argument, is very much on his best behaviour with Yahweh; the Samaritan woman is what might be described as devoutly impertinent with Jesus. The point is more clearly brought out in his encounter with the Syro-Phoenician woman (Mark 7.25-30; Matthew 15.21-8). And the point is of overriding practical import: that honest, devout, but heart-to-heart argument with God is the secret of petition.

The story of Zacchaeus must serve simply as another illustration of the encounter-prayer principle, for it, too, has an ascetical theological content (Luke 19.3-10). One encounters the Lord, not by Pelagian exercises, but by getting to the right place and waiting, getting into the right mood and watching. One does not seek Jesus, he seeks us, and calls: the little story is full of the doctrine of prevenient grace, which is the foundation of all prayer. So how do you get into the right place and mood? We are right in the thick of the spiritual theological field, with its supporting ascetic. The Gospels may appear to say little directly about prayer; they certainly contain no carefully worked out theories, methods or techniques. But there are plenty of encounters between man and God and here is another mine from which a New Testament ascetic may be quarried.

St Paul introduces the final stage: baptismal incorporation into the sacred humanity—the heart of Cistercian spirituality. But while the theological consequences of this are constantly studied throughout the ages, its treatment as source of interior life is comparatively rare, with the possible exception of Cistercian and later medieval extra-liturgical cult. This is mostly the extreme of affective devotion with little positive guidance for the spiritual director. What is 'incarnational' prayer?

At a stage or two removed, however, there is a wealth of practical meaning to be discovered from it. The great Pauline phrase 'in Christ' lies behind all prayer of the world-affirmation type which employs material things as devotional media; the visual contemplation of icon or crucifix, the tactile element in the rosary, even the sound of liturgical music, may be enriched by the application of this theology. It was what Chesterton was getting at when he said that mystical experience is something like the taste of an apple.

It is also concerned with the whole range of liturgical movement and devotional posture, with breathing discipline as in the Orthodox Jesus-prayer, and above all with habitual recollection in the human world.

There is much to be done. The immediate point is to insist that spiritual direction, based upon ascetical theology, is no medieval invention of academic artificiality. Although more developed doctrine, as biblical distillation as it were, plays a larger part in the on-the-slab process, it is all possessed of the firmest biblical foundation.

Chapter 9

Creed and Doctrine

STRAIGHT-DOWN-THE-LINE distinctions, plus an assessment of cultural factors, plus knowledge, plus love, all point to the fundamental approach by director to client. It is the starting point of the botanist's Flora analogy: analysis by elimination. But it is only a start: so far we have reduced our client's possible species, genus, variety and strain, by 75 per cent. Of a hundred possibles we know that he is not 75 of them. But 25 possibilities remain, and he must end up as dearly-beloved-in-the-Lord Thomas of unique individuality.

1. Creation

It is convenient to begin with the doctrine of creation because this is at the heart of our second straight-down-the-line distinction: world-affirmation or wide sacramentalism, against world-renunciation or *via negativa*. It also places everything in its existential pastoral setting, and introduces us to our client as theology describes him: the Christian doctrine of man.

Contemporary psychology has come full circle, back to the biblical conception of man as an integrated whole, a complex synthesis, who cannot be split up into isolatable characteristics or faculties. St Augustine saw this when he described man as made in the image of God in the form of trinity-in-unity, and when he interpreted sin as concupiscence; the disintegration of personality. But later, pastoral and moral theology began to suffer from what I have elsewhere called the Pygmalion image, arising out of a too literal interpretation of Genesis 2.7: 'And the Lord God formed man of the dust of the ground, and breathed into his nostrils the breath of life; and man became a living soul.' The false idea is that God, having moulded the statue and brought it to life, then

64

implanted certain fixed characteristics into a sort of static soul-substance. The misuse of the awkward word 'soul' does not help, which is one reason why it is here rejected in favour of 'client'.

The older moral theology is particularly prone to this kind of thinking. Virtue and grace are described as being acquired—tacked on to the statue—or infused; one imagines a hypodermic syringe injecting doses of faith, hope, and love into the soul-substance. The older theology of ordination follows the pattern when it talks of priestly character being stamped indelibly upon the soul, as if it were a putty-like substance ready to receive the sacerdotal seal squashed on to it. 'Conscience' too often sounds like a semi-physical organ; a lax one resembling a jellified kidney and a scrupulous one being something like a muscle with cramp.

Nobody, the psychologist least of all, thinks like that any more. Humanity is rather conceived as a flux of potentiality, of integrated movement towards a goal—authenticity, to use the jargon. Professor Macquarrie explains the concept fully and in theological context in *Principles of Christian Theology*, pp.64-74. 'Existence fulfils itself in selfhood. An authentic self is a unitary, stable, and relatively abiding structure in which the polarities of existence are held in balance and its potentialities are brought to fulfilment' (p.64).

At this point the synthesis-analysis conflict reappears in a different form. If modern psychology is concerned with integration, wholeness, complete personality, is not our directional insistence on the analytic cold slab out-of-date and unrealistic? Is the process even possible? If there are no fixed, substantial characteristics in our client, can he be analysed at all?

The fact is the reverse. Contemporary ways of looking at the doctrine of man enhance and support the whole process of spiritual direction. For if virtues, graces and gifts are substantial things 'infused' into a substantial soul-substance, then they are there, and there is little that can be done about it. But if they are potentialities, tendencies, seedlings, then they are to be nurtured and developed. If an honest man is someone whose static character has a large lump of honesty implanted into it, then that is the end of the matter. If, on the other hand, we are talking of an instinctive tendency, an *attrait*, towards honest dealing, something that can increase or decline, grow or die, then directorial nurture becomes very important indeed. And the same goes for tendencies and potentialities toward the speculative or the affective, towards affirmation or renunciation, towards this or that sort of prayer. A contemplative is not someone with certain fixed characteristics which give him an irrevocable status, but someone with an *attrait*, an inclination, towards contemplative prayer.

The wider doctrine of creation is of ascetical significance to both the affirming and the renunciative. To the former as vehicle for the divine disclosure, as mandala-symbol, implied in the sanctification of the senses. Creation as symbol is a favourite topic amongst the saints of the affirmative schools; Hugh of St Victor constructed a comprehensive system of prayer upon the doctrine. On the other side, the dangers of over-reacting to this propensity are obvious enough, and guard must ever be kept: laxity, self-indulgence, and worst of all immanental distortion, need to be kept in check. The renunciative must also be subjected to the doctrine of creation, especially in the avoidance of the heresy of angelism. To repeat, the reasoning runs that if God and the angels do not eat and sleep, then the less I eat and sleep the more like the angels I become, and so nearer to God. But we are not supposed to be angels, ever; we are destined to be sanctified human beings.

Creation applies to both types, indeed to every type, with regard to its two main derivatives. The first is the doctrine of divine providence, which follows from creation in that it implies the continuance of God's sabbath rest: creation is no simple fiat but a continuous process, ever sustained by the love of God. Events in the world, whether historical or personal, are therefore to be interpreted in spiritual terms. Again there is a vast literature on the theme of prayer as response to providence, of which the work of J. B. Bossuet, popularized by Jean de Caussade, is probably the best known.

The second derivative—if so it can be called—is St Thomas Aquinas' theory of a hierarchy of being. It is misleading and destructive of Christian prayer to misinterpret the notion of man as 'lord of creation'. He is lord of the known world, possibly of the universe, but certainly not of the creation which contains cherubim, seraphim, angels and archangels, the whole company of heaven embracing the saints of the Church triumphant and the inhabitants of paradise. In football terms, man is top of the third division not of the first. The doctrine is important in practice, for without it there will be over-stress on immanence, and consequently an inadequate conception of the transcendence of God. The approach to the incarnation will also suffer from distortion and reduction, and all incarnational prayer will suffer with it.

2. *Triune Being: the Holy Trinity*

The doctrine of creation is probably considered first because it describes our client within the context of his environment, thus giving spiritual direction a concrete base from which to operate.

The doctrine of God the Holy and undivided Trinity, however, is the key to the whole process. Far from being a metaphysical conundrum of interest only to the academician and of no practical consequence, it is the most down-to-earth spiritual formula that the Church has ever come up with. Neither progress nor spiritual health is possible without it, and it is the director's map and compass: the carpenter's saw, the surgeon's scalpel, the weaver's loom.

Christian prayer, which is the only springboard for Christian action, is controlled by the Trinity; the hallmark of Christian sanctity, the core of the Christian outlook on life, that which distinguishes it from any other religious system, is that it is trinitarian.

The substantive, that is the patristic and scholastic, formula, Father, Son, and Holy Spirit, is activated into attention to the divine transcendence, mediation through incarnation, and immanence; and from thence into the discernment of providential activity, redemptive love, and intuitive inspiration. The Christian ideal is a synthetic balance between these practical triads: transcendent prayer, adoration, praise and thanksgiving, precludes anxiety in a world which is insignificant compared with the glorious majesty of God. That is the importance of being top of the third division rather than bottom of the first. Yet, paradoxically— for the faith is all paradox—the incarnate mediation, sacrifice and redemption of the Son, points to a loving care and concern for all things: everything matters because of Christ and yet nothing matters except for Christ. And all the while, God, the majestically transcendent, wholly-other God, the real all-glorious God, is immanent in all creation, in every person. Through the indwelling Spirit, our silly little life in this silly little world becomes all important from an eternal perspective.

The ideal of Christian life comes from a synthetic balance between these triads; transcendence precludes anxiety, immanence involves action on both natural and supernatural planes, and the mediation of the Son points to a joyful, loving care for all things. A large amount of spiritual direction is concerned with the creation and sustenance of this balanced perspective. Distortion arises from over and under stresses on one side or the other of the trinitarian synthesis. The ascetical aspects of all this have been worked out in the minutest detail, covering hundreds of pages of the basic textbooks. Repetition would be tedious and out of place in this practical discussion. But for completeness, the bare bones are clear enough: overstress on transcendence leads to formalism, legalism—getting stuck in the covenant stage of prayer—and ultimately deism, which is the pitfall of the speculative type. Overstress on immanence produces subjectivism, quasi-mysticism that exaggerates the importance of religious experience, the wrong sort of worldliness and then pantheism.

The paradoxical balance is reproduced in the relation between manhood and Godhead in the incarnate Son: the Redeemer to be adored and the redeemer to be embraced; the compassionate healer and the sacrificial Lamb. Care must be taken over the adjective 'christo-centric' which has both valid and invalid connotations. If Christ is central to the Trinity, the fulcrum and focus between Father and Spirit, then all is well, but when the emphasis is on Jesus to the exclusion, or diminution of Father and Spirit then all is decidedly not well.

Since no one ever gets the balance exactly right, these stresses and counter-stresses point to an elaboration of the original down-the-line distinctions. Does the client's natural *attrait* tend towards the majesty of the Father almighty? Or towards the comforting presence of the indwelling Spirit? Or is it spontaneously led to affective devotion to the incarnate Son? Are these tendencies gifts to be developed or distortions to be curbed? In the directorial interview, these are prior questions, and not always easy questions, with which the director is concerned.

The traditional way of creating this healthy balance, or the nearest we can hope to get to it, is the Benedictine *regula*: the daily inter-relation between divine office, holy eucharist, and personal prayer. Millions of words of commentary have been expended on this scheme, which it would be again superfluous to repeat. Suffice it to mention that this time-honoured system is under considerable criticism from both contemporary theology and changing cultural patterns. From the first it is too analytic, too regimented, insufficiently free and adventurous; from the second it is deemed to be artificial, monkish, ghetto-minded, and formal—duty over freedom. Be that as it may. The gigantic challenge confronting the critic is that he is called upon to invent a substitute which is thoroughly theological and deeply trinitarian, which works in the sense of creating the Christian outlook on, and in, life, which the *regula* is well proven to do. A hotchpotch of devotions which look more attractive is not enough; we are concerned with theological foundations which issue in Christian life and work.

We are dealing with prayer, the end-product of which is that Christian influence and service which aims at the redemption of the world, no less. And it is here that the significance of the trinitarian formula is overlooked, for if the emphasis is on immanence exclusively, on social justice, economic policies, political action, then the Church is bound to fail. It is only the transcendent emphasis that gives these things point; otherwise we have moved from the top of the third division to the bottom of the fourth.

The ancient formula remains essential in direction, while the more synthetic, existential formula of Triune Being gives a better idea of the trinitarian God to be worshipped. You cannot worship a formula; only the underlying reality to which it leads, but without the formula the reality is unlikely to be reached. Without the map one is liable to get lost.

3. *Christology*

Every Christian has the notion that the person of Jesus Christ combines divine and human elements, and many of the faithful are content to leave it at that. Contemporary theology continues to speculate upon the mystery, often in a manner richly pertinent to christological prayer. The emphasis, as might be expected, is on the God-man, Jesus Christ, in his whole, integrated Being, ascended, glorified, and yet ever present. You still cannot worship, adore, or communicate with a formula, yet modern christology is such that transference from formula to reality is comparatively straight-forward.

But the spiritual director needs different tools, and he will find himself thrown back upon the ancient Definition of Chalcedon. He will also find that concentration on the notorious errors, the rejection of which created the doctrine, is a very positive exercise indeed. This is not to accept Chalcedon uncritically, to adopt an ultra-conservative stick-in-the-mud stance, rejecting all more recent developments. It is rather a search through the toolbag, looking for precisely the most appropriate implements for the job in hand: and here they are. From the director's point of view, with his client on the stone cold slab, Chalcedon poses exactly the right questions.

In terms of living prayer, not necessarily of intellectual belief, how does the client approach Jesus Christ? What does he assume, consciously or sub-consciously, when he contemplates the crucifix? What does he make of the central figure as he meditates on the Gospel narrative? Is Jesus lovingly and comfortably human? Is he remotely, mysteriously, frighteningly divine? Or does he alternate between the two: God in the Eucharist and man in the street? Or is he a muddled mixture of both? Above all is Jesus Christ ever isolated from Father and Spirit; or is he in some curious way roughly the same as one or the other or both?

These questions show that the musty old heresies that underlie Chalcedon die hard, they recur in practically every directorial interview, and they offer invaluable guidelines about our client's prayer, thence his life, thence his Christian influence on the world. No reasonably well-informed Christian would hold to any of these errors, none would fail to recognize them as errors, yet in prayer, in life, in service, they inveigle their way in.

The Arian-Apollinarian imbalance is the core of this aspect of the process, and it presents a curious reversal of attitude as between contemporary theology and the prayer of the faithful. Arianism, or quasi-Arianism is the constant danger for modern christology, and not a few theologians of eminence have gone frighteningly near to it. Cultural fashion could be the instigator, since emphasis on the Church's social task, on a practical this-worldliness, seen as its direct mission, puts all the stress on the human and humanitarian nature of Jesus. His divinity is either slurred over or seen as a piece of theoretical metaphysic of no immediate consequence. This is not to deny the importance of the Church's social mission, but to insist that it cannot be a direct man-made programme. It can only be pursued *via* prayer, which needs a Chalcedonian type christology, otherwise mission has no power and theology no spiritual content. Christological prayer demands a divine nature, and on the whole, the praying faithful are well aware of that.

Apollinarianism, on the other hand, though theologically in the doldrums, is by far the greater danger to contemporary prayer. Without the fullness of human nature, the third stage of the biblical progression—incorporation in Christ—becomes impossible and meaningless, yet this is the crux of affirmative contemplation in the world. The Apollinarian client tends toward some sort of Manichaean tension, distrusting the senses and ashamed of life's rightful joys; an *affective* attrait turns towards sentimentality—the Cross is slightly unreal—and eucharistic devotion loses its bite.

When these erroneous tendencies are put to rights, health is restored and growth assured, and they can be countered in various ways. To the speculative type, straight teaching of Chalcedonian christology helps a great deal; and maintenance of the basic trinitarian balance by *regula* or some other means is of assistance. If congenial, imaginative meditation on the Gospel narratives—especially those of encounter—restores christological balance.

Otherwise ascetic disciplines may come to our aid. Rejection of the Apollinarian heresy incites the affirmative client to sanctify the senses and interpret creation in the sense of St Irenaeus' recapitulation theology: all material things have their place in the redemptive process; the world is lifted up into God. The bodily functions, food, drink, sex, become sanctified, sacramental, and worthy of profound respect. The renunciative client may properly follow the sacrificial and penitential emphases of his state, a sharing of the sufferings of the sacred humanity, but he is guarded against angelism and its corollaries by taking Chalcedon seriously. In both cases, do not overdo it!

The Nestorian error—the divine Christ in the eucharist and the human Jesus in the street—is important for obvious reasons. It leads to the sort of sanctuary-centred devotion which those suspicious of spiritual guidance rightly fear. It fails in service and mission, not because it begins in the wrong place but because it ends there, and it fails to give due honour to the blessed sacrament because it stops short at regular communion without its leading into eucharistic life. Here there is a sacred-secular divorce, leading into a sort of spiritual schizophrenia.

Today it is culturally destructive because, even amongst the faithful, it tends to the Pelagian error already indicated: social service, works of charity and true Christian influence can only arise out of prayer. Devotion is sterile when it is founded upon a Nestorian Christ. The practice of eucharistic recollection—the Jesus prayer and suchlike—combats the error, as also does honest, argumentative colloquy: the prayer of encounter. So do many other things, for it all depends on the client.

The point is that trinitarian doctrine, and christology which grows from it, particularly in its patristic and scholastic forms, produce the tools for competent guidance; especially to start with, but to be kept in constant readiness thereafter. But tools are to be used, not described and talked about. My client turns out to be a speculative-transcendental-Christo-centric, with Apollinarian leanings and Benedictine *attrait*: dear old Thomas. It is not of much use to tell him that, or to talk to him in that sort of jargon, but it is essential for the director to think in that sort of jargon. I do not want medical science from my doctor, but I hope he understands it himself, and because he does I want him to tell me what to do: I have a sprained ankle, do I rest or exercise it? Thomas has a nasty dose of aridity, does he plod on or give up? He does not want to know what Scaramelli thought about it, or the intricacies of the Salesian solution: his director does.

The monophysite heresy, to complete the picture, is where we came in at the start of this section; it is the prevalent devout muddle that ascribes both humanity and divinity to Jesus Christ and leaves it at that. Like a child's chicken-pox it is not very serious, but it should not be there and it is better watched.

Meantime christology moves in various directions; sometimes in ways detrimental to spiritual progress, sometimes offering new insights which assist it. The spiritual director has to keep pace in a discriminating way, but because of the cultural factor, keep pace he must. To see the usefulness of ancient and venerable formulae is not to be ultra-conservative or blind to change. If someone improves on the garden spade I will take serious note, but until he does I keep with my trusted old favourite. On the other hand I would not be happy if my doctor produced a bottle of leeches.

I am not here concerned with doctrinal exposition, ancient or modern, but with attempting to demonstrate how doctrine is forged into directorial tools. This is why the fundamental statements of the creeds have been grouped under the headings of creation, trinity, and christology. The remaining clauses are to be grouped in a similar way. All such groupings are artificial and arbitrary because finally the faith forms a synthetic whole, so a good deal of overlapping is to be expected. In context, however, the concern is with those groupings which best serve the purpose of direction.

4. *The Atonement and the Last Things*

This heading could as easily have been placed under Moral Theology in the next chapter, since the client's attitude to, and interpretation of, atonement doctrine determines his moral stance. The Last Things are conveniently coupled with atonement doctrine since teleology—the final aim and end of human endeavour—is one of the distinguishing marks of Christian, as opposed to secular, ethics.

It is common knowledge that there is no dogmatic formula to explain the fact of atonement, and the various explanations propounded by the fathers are roughly divisible into objective and subjective theories; the former regarding the Cross as a divine fiat of redemption, and the latter as a moral example to stir up penitence as prerequisite of forgiveness. It is a problem that has troubled the Church since St Paul posed the question: 'Shall we then sin that grace may abound?' 'God forbid', and what follows in Romans 6 is more of an exhortation than a rational answer.

It is, nevertheless, an important distinction in direction since it corresponds to the speculative-affective division, and it is the basis for the important moral distinction between a lax and a scrupulous conscience. The speculative client, coolly intelligent and dutiful will more likely take the objective line: by the Cross the battle is won, in Christ redemption is assured; shall we then sin that grace may abound? Why not? Well not quite: temptation must be fought rationally and by grace, but there is no need to get worked up about it.

The affective client, on the other hand, is emotionally disturbed by the crucifixion and by the passion; if redemption is won, look at the cost! Or if it is still to be won—there is an honest doubt about it—then there is much to be done: self-examination, heart-searching, penitence, confession, and continual meditation on the passion narrative.

Carried to extremes, the former client could sin seriously without too much concern, while the latter risks a scrupulosity which casts doubt upon the efficacy of repentance, the reality of absolution, and even the wisdom of receiving Holy Communion.

The patristic doctrine, or lack of doctrine, on the atonement, is therefore more satisfactory to the spiritual director than it is to the systematic theologian. That there is no firm answer fits better with the former's job than with the latter's aspiration.

Correction of the foregoing distortions is an obvious need, and frequently an early one. The speculative-objective type needs to return to the Gospel accounts, preferably by meditation on the passion of our Lord. But if he has no vivid imagination, which may well be the case, pictures and films can be of considerable help. The central fact is that sin is utterly destructive of all values and of the whole life; it is not something extraneous to be simply got rid of. In such cases it is sometimes wise to counsel against frequent use of the sacrament of penance, insisting, after good Anglican precedent, upon thorough and regular self-examination and non-sacramental confession: it can be much more difficult!

Scrupulosity—if it really comes to that—is an intractable problem, but to oversimplify, the opposite counsel suggests itself for the affective-subjective client. Frequent confession, with stress upon its inviolability, and as much straight teaching from the Irenaeus-Anselm school of thought as such a client can absorb.

Our pattern here might be Julian of Norwich, whose *Revelations* brilliantly combine into an affective-speculative synthesis. Her description of the passion should stir the coldest while all is firmly rooted in the objectivity of Christ's redeeming act.

The atonement is closely linked with both of the original straight-down-the-line distinctions (see chapter 5): affirmation-renunciation as well as speculative-affective, together with the derivatives now being considered. The objective-speculative client is likely to combine an objective atonement outlook with heavy stress on the Fatherhood of God and the divinity of Christ. He will be happy with the covenant prayer-stage, with liturgy central to all other prayer. His counterpart is almost certainly Christo-centric, in either the proper or improper sense, with centrality given to imaginative meditation on the Gospels, stressing the divine humanity and concentrating on the Passion.

The distinction colours the life-stance perhaps more than any other. The speculative man lives under the shadow of the Cross, for he is a Christian, but it is the glorious and victorious Cross, pointing to the world which, despite appearances, has received the good news of redemption achieved. The affective lives under the shadow of the other Cross, the tense and terrifying Cross of tragedy. Once more Julian of Norwich indicates the ideal: the Cross is appalling, but because of it, all manner of thing shall be well. The affective symbol is the suffering Christ on the naked crucifix. The speculative emblem is Christus Rex.

Covenant-prayer and encounter-prayer are stressed on one or other of these distinctive sides, but incorporation remains the ideal for both. The doctrines of Resurrection and Ascension come in at this point, because in-Christ, both types of atonement-outlook are possible, and both are proved to be legitimate if unideal starting points. To be in-Christ must involve creative suffering and an element of subjective penitence; yet the speculative is also right, Christ reigns, despite appearances, through resurrection and ascension, and we are ascended and risen in him. The transcendent element can never be omitted.

The conventional Last Things of Advent support these observations: death and judgement deserve more consideration than they are wont to receive today, while the doctrines of Heaven and Hell, though in much need of serious re-evaluation, cannot be left out of a moral system which is both anthropological and teleological: in simple terms a system which initially asks what is man and what is he for? We are back with the recurrent cultural point: if the Church has a this-worldly mission, it cannot by-pass prayer and the transcendent.

5. *Church and sacraments*

If 1 Corinthians 9.24-7 is the seed from which ascetical theology springs, then 1 Corinthians 12 is something of a spiritual director's mandate. Direction is an individual, person-to-person business by which a wide diversity of gifts is discovered, nurtured and brought to fruition. But Christian individuality flourishes only within the unity of the Body, which in pastoral terms is its localized microcosm: the local Christian community. It can happen that a director's proper concern with individuality overshadows his client's essential membership of the Body corporate. This is not only a serious error in itself, but one which plays into the hands of those critics of direction who fear a self-centred, self-improving, ghetto mentality.

However much of a platitude, it must constantly be stated that there is no such thing as 'private' prayer. All prayer, however personal—which is not the same as private—is of the Church, and all prayer is of vicarious significance since the Church is the redemptive organism. The development of individual gifts is first and foremost service to the Church, and through the Church service to the world. It is those without competent guidance who are liable to be driven into a holy corner.

Another obvious division arises, of both psychological and ascetical importance; that between the gregarious and the solitary, or historically between coenobite and recluse. The overriding principle is that neither is dissociated from the Church, but both serve the Church in their distinctive ways. This raises the question of the subtle series of relations between spiritual director, his client, and his local community led by the parish priest.

The parochial strategy of a Christian community demands loyal support, but if there are diversities of gifts there needs to be flexibility. It is not always understood that any strategy, however evangelistic, outgoing and healthily objective, gains incalculably from the supportive prayer of the solitary. The individual gifts of God—talents—need to be doubled not buried, and pastoral strategy means using the tools one has, not bemoaning the fact that other tools are lacking. To look at the simplest example, a solitary, amateur-type parishioner might prefer said celebrations in the early morning to elaborate ritual at the parish eucharist. Such a one could be self-centred, anti-social, irresponsible and all the rest, which needs to be corrected, but he could also be exercising genuine *attrait* for and on behalf of the community. Spiritual direction cannot exclude consideration from both sides and its decisions can be delicate. The doctrine of the Church, especially the aspects outlined in 1 Corinthians 12, has much bearing upon the guidance of each individual: there has to be balance between diversities of gifts and the unity of the Body.

Life in the Church means the sacramental life; the common and binding factor within all of our categories, classifications, and divisions. But there are still variables in approach and practice, aspects of sacramental doctrine which are of particular relevance to direction. There is, for example, the question of frequency of Holy Communion: the speculative, objective-atonement type of person may wish to communicate daily, and why not? Jesus said do this, so do it, and without a lot of affective, penitential, and other preparatory devotions: why all the fuss? It is all part of the game. The opposite sort of man, subjective, emotional, scrupulous, will exercise much more caution, requiring very serious preparation, self-examination, and confession of some costing kind. Is the eucharist the Christian's daily food or is it the most precious of all God's gifts to be savoured sparingly? It must be both; there are no plain rights and wrongs, but possible distortion from both sides. It is a question of *attrait*, and how often a particular client should communicate is not quite the simple question it looks.

Another point of doctrine is that the Eucharist is, autonomously and within itself, the supreme intercession for every possible occasion. It does not preclude personal intercession of the usual kind, especially for those specially gifted in this respect, but it can be of much importance to those without specific intercessory gifts. These latter are not excused normal intercession, but it may be reduced to a simple minimum and replaced by eucharistic action seen as intercessory. Following *attrait* does not mean ascetical hedonism, neither does it imply the glossing over of everything difficult; it does not preclude struggle and yet there is little virtue in plodding away at something for which one is innately unfitted, while neglecting one's proper gifts. There is little point in spending laborious hours teaching the opening batsman how to bowl: it is not his job within the team.

The same principle applies more obviously to frequency of sacramental confession with the distinction of speculative-objective on the one hand and affective-subjective on the other, leading into their derivative types of conscience: probably, if not necessarily, laxity or scrupulosity as tendencies.

There can be no rule-of-thumb, but in general frequency of confession varies inversely as between these types: often for the lax, less often for the scrupulous. Yet dear Thomas still refuses to fit neatly into a theoretical slot. Theory offers guidelines while the real directorial disaster is some blanket viewpoint that, whether in the Eucharist or the confessional, the more frequent the better.

The sacrament of reconciliation will generally play some part in direction, but it need not, and its place will be a comparatively minor one: a handy little tool at the bottom of the bag. The equation of direction with confession is the serious error.

6. *The Communion of Saints*

The doctrine of the Communion of Saints follows from that of the Church three-fold; the Church militant ever points to the Church triumphant. The ascetical function of the doctrine is to offer a valuable safeguard against immanentalism, while somewhat softening the transcendent aspect. Prayer means life in com-munion with the saints, on a higher than earthly plane, and yet such communion is not with metaphysical speculation but with people.

The doctrine is of importance to direction for two reasons. First, because it is the teaching and experience of the saints which gives rise to the schools of prayer that form the final part of the ascetical syllabus. It is here that all of our categories, analyses and on-the-slab distinctions become clothed with flesh and blood. Having reduced our client to species, genus, variety and strain, he can now be introduced to those saints—sanctified people—who can provide him with the most congenial spiritual environment: the school of his *attrait*. Needless to say, without the cold and clinical preliminaries, the quest for this correct environment amongst the vast complexity of Christian spirituality, would be a hit-or-miss affair of the needle-in-a-haystack kind. There would be no starting point.

Secondly, spiritual reading itself, that is the use of traditional writings and instruction, takes on a new meaning. The saints are our contemporaries, members of the same living Church, not distinguished old boys who died long ago. Their writings are also contemporary, so the distinction between ancient and modern, although of some usefulness, is not strictly accurate. To compare modern spiritual writing with that from the patristic and scholastic ages is to compare differences in expression and culture rather than of age. St Augustine becomes not so much an ancient writer but a contemporary one, who nevertheless uses an idiom and a cultural framework with which we may be unfamiliar. But he can still guide: the familiar story of the Orthodox seer who says, without affectation, that Gregory Palamas told him this morning . . . expresses a profound truth.

The doctrine of the three-fold Church lies behind this reading-praying technique, and it is bound up with the doctrines of Resurrection and Ascension: it is the risen and glorified Christ into whom we are baptismally incorporated. This worldly-otherworldly balance is at the heart of Christian prayer, cutting across the affirmation-renunciative distinction. The world, including the Church Militant, is real, good and conducive to prayer, yet it can only be served and redeemed when prayer transcends it.

Chapter 10

Moral Theology

ONE OF THE most pressing needs for spiritual direction is for a marriage, or at least a dialogue, between moral theology and Christian ethics. In recent times the latter has tended to replace the former, and for various reasons. It may be seen primarily as part of a secularization process necessitated by cultural change. Moral theology, based on the biblical revelation and theological concepts, has come to be regarded, rightly or wrongly, as legalistic, authoritarian, and too narrowly conceived to make any impact upon a pluralistic society.

Christian ethics, on the other hand, is seen as one aspect of moral philosophy, which logically gives it a more general authority. This is all to the good, and serious work in this field has given ethical theism a far more reputable place in the general scheme of contemporary thought than it has enjoyed for some time. Moreover the alliance, such as it is, between New Testament and theological concepts with wider ethical systems and classifications, could give those added insights into traditional moral theology which the spiritual director badly needs. The marriage is needed by both sides and the continuing courtship is to be welcomed.

From the director's point of view, however, Christian ethics cannot be sufficient. Its main failure is in its inadequacy of guidance for personal choice, which raises a curious series of anomalies. Objective, normative type theories can come up with fairly clear-cut judgements on particular issues, but with little concern for personal decision in a unique situation. Christian ethics indeed may come up with those 'blanket judgements' against which 'traditional' Christian morality is unjustly accused. On the other hand, existential-situation ethics, with all of the emphasis on personal choice within the unique situation, offers little positive guidance as to how such choice is to be made responsibly.

A clear-cut decision about contraception, for example, does not preclude personal decision of conscience in a particular situation, and decision-making guidance—casuistry—is required. To make some universal principle like 'love' the sole criterion of choice does not help either, because, in this situation, 'love' can equally well be expressed either way. That circumstances alter cases is no new invention but the foundation of traditional casuistry, and it is some such system that this type of ethical theory needs before it makes practical sense. Here is a possibility of Christian ethics and moral theology in creative interaction.

At first sight moral theology may look forbidding and unreal. Like ascetical theology all of its subtle categories, distinctions between types of sin and virtue, and intricate gradations of guilt and gravity; all of this looks cold, clinical and artificial. It can even appear impious; if sin is rejection of the will of God, if its price is the Cross of Christ, then dare we make legalistic distinctions of this kind? Is not sin sin? Is not love love? Is not faith faith? Are such virtues and vices consonant with the principle of moderation, of kind and degree?

This is the kind of criticism which makes moral theology suspect and which plays a part in its rejection in favour of Christian ethics. It is parallel with the suspicion that has also haunted ascetical theology: is not prayer a simple, childlike thing? Is not Christian living a simple devotion to Jesus? Why all the fuss? But in both cases this criticism is based on a false assumption as to what these studies are for. It is assumed that both ascetics and moral theology are to be taught in general rather than applied in personal direction.

There is something of a parallel as between the interaction of ancient doctrinal formulae and contemporary reinterpretation in ascetics, and between moral theology and Christian ethics. In both cases the newer studies are of value for straight teaching, for enlightenment and understanding by contemporary people, while the older writings form the basic tools of the directorial trade. If modern christologies help to introduce the living Jesus, the old Chalcedonian categories remain as necessary tools for the prayerful furtherance of that relationship. Similarly, if Christian ethics offers acceptable moral systems and principles to modern people, it is the categories of moral theology that the director needs for guidance. Christian ethics could argue persuasively that abortion is wrong but that circumstances alter cases; only moral theology can interpret that in terms of personal decision within a practical situation.

There would appear to be some hope for a creative marriage between Christian ethics and moral theology, as there is between contemporary theology and its patristic and scholastic ancestors. But we cannot evade the dissimilarities, and in some aspects conflict. There are certain qualities in moral theology which distinguish it from any other ethical system, and which even Christian ethics does not always recognize. The fundamental distinction is that just considered: the question of purpose. Christian ethics attempts, most worthily, to give moral philosophical substance and general acceptance to the Christian viewpoint, and latterly it has done its job very well. Moral theology is concerned to produce tools for Christian living, more especially as they are employed in spiritual direction, and this without undue concern about what society at large feels about it. The marriage is still desirable but the distinctiveness of moral theology should be plainly recognized and plainly stated.

Moral theology is anthropological, it concerns the doctrine of man, and at this first point many contemporary ethicists, even avowedly secular ones, will applaud, for general ethical thought is moving in this direction: what is man and what is he for?

But moral theology comes up with an answer that is not so generally acceptable: the teleological answer. Man is for the beatific vision which is his ultimate target, and there can be no other consideration. Man's last end, not the wellbeing of society or the initiation of universal justice, or even love between neighbours, is the one criterion for moral judgement. The Christian good is not that which promotes happiness or reduces suffering or initiates justice, but directs men towards the vision of God. Christian ethics can give us a lead on abortion but it gets bewildered by the contemplative life of a recluse. It is at this point that world affirmation and *via negativa* spirituality meet in a common aspiration. The one affirms the values of creation for eternal ends, seeing things as vehicles for the divine disclosure, and looking towards their final glory in God. The other renounces material things for precisely the same reason, to give undivided attention to

God as his way to the beatific vision. Moral philosophy has little to offer to the pursuit of these values.

This teleological basis of moral theology is but the final stage of a longer process, and constitutes the ultimate divergence of values. But such divergence becomes more and more apparent as spiritual life advances. Most systems of ethics, including the strictly secular, are happy enough with the cardinal virtues: justice, temperance, fortitude and prudence are universal values. Faith, hope and love might be fitted in to some systems, but certainly not all, and when we reach the gifts of the Spirit the divorce is plain. This extraordinary list of the higher Christian virtues, properly interpreted, contains qualities which play a minimal part in Christian ethics and which would be excluded altogether from most secular systems.

Moral theology also includes virtues which are directly related to the *askesis* which is supportive of prayer and which therefore assists progress towards the ultimate end. Qualities such as humility, meekness and abandonment might enter ethical schemes of a stoic type, and they may be squeezed into Christian ethics in a roundabout way, but this would be a strained and artificial process. Christian ethics is happy enough with almsgiving, but it could make little of fasting, mortification and the like disciplines, yet these are essential elements of moral theology. The gap widens still further when penitence, by typical Christian paradox, becomes the positive and joyful virtue that moral theology insists it is.

The crux comes with a more fundamental Christian paradox. Christian ethics is concerned with the bases of moral philosophy, with the good, beautiful and true, with right and wrong, is and ought. It comes up with reasoned conclusions about current moral issues: sexual ethics, nationalism, race relations, finance, work, nuclear power and all the rest. Moral theology makes the same attempt at solving the same problems, and frequently arrives at the same answers. But having ascertained what, in a particular situation, the right course of action is, moral theology immediately insists that fallen man is incapable of pursuing that right course. Ethics says this is what you ought to do: full stop. Moral theology says this is what you ought to do: but you cannot.

Before this seeming brick wall, grace has to be taken seriously, which means that prayer and the sacraments enter moral issues. Prayer and morality become inseparable, which is something that

Christian ethics finds it difficult to deal with: ethic and ascetic are two sides of the same coin, and so fasting, mortification and the rest of the underlying *askesis* become moral as well as religious virtues. In itself there is nothing especially virtuous about fasting; disciplined response by *regula* has little or no value to moral philosophy, but to moral theology it is the very spring of action.

Ethics, Christian or secular, claims autonomy; it purports to be something in its own right, a *sui generis* discipline and science. That is its strength, and when ethics of this kind is seen to support fundamental Christian concepts, as frequently it does, then we have valuable apologetic. But moral theology cannot claim such autonomy, for Christian morality is not only inseparable from prayer and grace but it is subservient to them. Moral endeavour, guided by moral theology, is the test rather than the means of spiritual progress.

The Christian ethics-moral theology marriage remains desirable, and there are signs that it may be possible. Contemporary ethics, for example, stresses the centrality of choice in moral judgements: 'decision is king' according to H. Aitkin. John Macquarrie takes up this concept in relation to the doctrine of creation, which involves risk on the part of the Creator, loving risk indeed but risk nevertheless. Risk, therefore, becomes something of a divine attribute, a positive and courageous thing rather than a misfortune. Such a concept supports traditional casuistry, and especially its probabilist centre, against rigorist theories. Probabilism might be described as the theory of trust God and take a chance, but if choice is the centre of the new ethic, then some guidance is required as to how such decision is to be made: casuistry is essential.

Situation ethics supports the same conclusion: circumstances alter cases, each situation is unique, so every personal decision is unique. But there must be guiding principles and it is now generally agreed that the overall principle of love is too simplistic as a practical guide: how do you love a naughty child; with caresses or punishment? Which, ultimately, is the more 'loving'? When the ambiguities of love are ironed out we are back to more workable principles that look very much like old-fashioned probabilism.

But the marriage is certainly not complete, and in the meantime spiritual direction is forced to follow the same theological double course; keeping abreast with all that is best in Christian ethical studies while at the same time reverting to the analytic categories of traditional moral theology.

Judged by the synthetic, existential approach of modern ethical philosophy, these classifications appear to be old-fashioned and artificial, as does Chalcedon compared with contemporary christology. But the same point applies: we need the latter to make the living Christ present and real; the former still supplies the tools for direction. The distinction needs to be made and clearly understood, and much criticism of the older system is allayed so soon as it is realized precisely what the classifications are *for*.

Set over against the Christian ethicist, or even the philosophical moralist, the spiritual director has to use the map of moral progress as guide and test of spiritual progress. He must study the ascetical place of the cardinal virtues, the theological virtues, and the gifts of the Spirit. He needs to classify types of conscience in order that individual conscience may be guided and trained. Conscience otherwise degenerates into emotivism; so we are again grateful to Christian ethicists for constructing a theory of emotivism and generally condemning it, because it has played havoc, and remains a bugbear, to Christian moral thinking. It is well to have it pointed out that 'I am sure God wishes me to do this' and 'my conscience says that I must do that' are statements on the level with 'Guinness is good for you'. Such assurances may be true or false, but they cannot carry much authority.

Most controversial of all, the spiritual director has to have, in the back of his head, to be applied not taught, distinctions and classifications of sin, and these are so complicated that charges of artificiality appear to be more than reasonable. But the ultimate question remains: what is it all *for*? To guide prayer, to deepen the relationship between man and God in Christ, to assist progress towards man's last end. At first sight, contour lines on a map do not seem to bear much relation to the scenery, or to be of much help in choosing the route towards one's destination. Properly interpreted they have much to do with both.

As a subsection of moral philosophy, Christian ethics claims to be an objective, autonomous science, and that is its weakness. Moral theology is a branch of theology, so it is subservient to theology as such; it is handmaid to ascetic, playing a significant but minor role in the total process of Christian living, and that is its strength. Christianity is not moralism: it is religion.

So moral theology has to be underpinned by wider theological concepts: grace, atonement, redemption, penitence, prayer, incarnational existence. It is a question of the priorities that any sort of ethics has to give to the moral implications of this world; social justice, community relations, political theory and the like. Moral theology is unashamedly concerned with man's last end and his attainment thereof. It assumes that man is *in via*, on the way, and it is concerned with the destination as well as the journey towards that end. Christian ethics may help to make the map: only moral theology can tell each unique human being how to make the journey.

Chapter 11

The Schools

WITH OUR CLIENT on the slab, we have now unearthed a skeleton list of opposing tendencies: speculative-affective; renunciative-affirming; transcendence-immanence; Father-Christo-centrism-Holy Spirit; lax-scrupulous conscience; objective-subjective atonement theory; extrovert-introvert; Arian-Apollinarian; individual-corporate; recluse-gregarious; active-passive; amateur-professional; grim-gay; upper class-lower class.

The possible computations within this all too simple list are quite beyond my mathematical competence, but it all helps to reduce our client to a manageable type: genus, species, variety and strain. Because our clients are people they will be awkward and muddle up the neatness of this sort of pattern. Extrovert Thomas who holds to the objectivity of atonement ought to incline to laxity of conscience; but he turns out to be the reverse. Amateur-affective-affirming Jenny ought to be happy in the kitchen contemplating a cabbage; she probably rushes off to church at every opportunity in a cloak that makes her look like a nun. You can never tell with people, which, despite the necessary slab, is what our clients persist in being. But we have now something solid to build on.

Human illogicality breathes life into the bare bones on the slab, and it is the living wisdom of the ages and of the saints that breathes life into ascetical theology. We look to the schools of spirituality to clothe the whole process of direction with flesh and blood. 'The diversity of the saints baffles analysis,' wrote Alban Goodier, and so do the schools of prayer associated with them. Any attempt to classify must be of the simplest and most general kind, with the exceptions often obscuring the rule. The Dominicans, on the whole, are well over on the speculative side, while Aquinas himself wrote deeply affective hymns, and the little Rhineland Branch of the order went way over on the *via negativa* side. The

Cistercians, by and large, affirm creation and centre their all on the sacred humanity, but they can also be pretty tough on mortification. There is a thread, a hallmark, a central characteristic which marks off one school from another, but the whole story of the development of the tradition, with its interactions, dependencies, family relationships and contradictions, is of immense complexity.

Such studies of the schools have been made over and over again, and they are an important part of the spiritual director's armoury, but they are only a beginning: there can be no substitute for first-hand acquaintance, both as foundation to ascetical studies and also as the material for inspiration in prayer itself. An examination of the theological foundations of a school is important to ascetical studies, but ultimately one has to taste it: what we have said about the communion of saints is the key; St Bernard really can speak to us, guide us, here and now.

It is sometimes said that theological students read so many commentaries on the Scriptures that they never get round to reading the Bible, and ascetics is sometimes in danger of the same error. So taste and see.

The direction of a client into the right school for him, the guidance given for spiritual reading as living basis of a life of prayer, is one of the most difficult tasks a spiritual director has to face. There is still the balance to be considered between the proper development of *attrait* and the curbing of its distortion by excess. Untold harm can come from the indiscriminate use of a conglomeration of holy books. No one wishes to curb devotion or exercise the wrong sort of authoritarianism; no Christian, certainly no Anglican, can be forbidden to read what he likes. But guidance is necessary on two levels; first as to which school, which of the saints, is likely to be the most constructive guide for a particular client, and secondly, some introduction and explanation as to the fundamental outlook and emphasis on that school or saint. If one reads the leading article of a newspaper it is as well to know a little about the editor's political slant and the paper's editorial policy.

We are involved in the theology of the double vocation, in its application to secular clients. The primary vocation of a would-be religious is simply to be a religious, to offer his life to God in that particular way. His secondary vocation is to a particular order, embracing a specific school. And the choice is a delicate one, often made only after years of experiment; a postulant of Benedictine *attrait* would not fare too well in a Franciscan friary. To a lesser degree, the same applies to seculars, who also need guidance into the right school, but here the choice is even more difficult since the secular client is not confronted with an overpowering ethos which is obviously either right or wrong for him. He can go on for a long time in less intense yet equally destructive frustration.

The spiritual life of the director follows the same pattern, also of course under direction, but he needs to acquire a much wider knowledge of the schools if he is to guide those who are different from himself. Confronted with this enormous mass of complicated literature, where, and how, does he begin? It might be worthwhile to attempt some sort of systematic approach to this gigantic and never-ending job.

The first step might be to master a comparatively concise commentary on the history and development of Christian spirituality, if only to bring some sort of order and shape into the exercise. It is of assistance to see how the schools arose and to look into their theological antecedents. The Cistercian emphasis on the sacred humanity, for example, follows the christology of St Irenaeus; St Benedict is influenced by the trinitarian doctrine of St Augustine; the Pseudo-Dionysian *via negativa* derives from the school of Alexandria, especially from the influence of Origen. All of which helps to stamp each school with its fundamental characteristics, and a rough pattern emerges out of what first looked like chaos.

Next it is necessary for the spiritual director to develop his own *attrait* by concentrating his own spiritual pilgrimage upon the school proper to it. He will then find himself to be different from most of his clients, but this should be accepted and declared. Psychoanalysts are generally willing to declare their position—they follow Freud, or Jung, or Adler, or Stekel—and if spiritual directors do the same then the client at least knows where he is, and in certain cases such knowledge and admission of bias may assist the directorial process.

The spiritual director now comes to his own particular, long-drawn-out, even laborious task; he must acquaint himself with a fair number of the main schools, and this from three different angles. The theology behind each school is to be studied, and its writings have to be analysed from this viewpoint. The same works should then be approached as spiritual reading, tasted, until the ethos is absorbed. Finally, and most difficult of all, the director has to experiment in prayer according to each school's method and technique, and this will run counter to his own personal *attrait*.

To plough through the four weeks of the Ignatian exercises, for one to whom that sort of thing is not specially suited, is a laborious experience indeed. Yet it is necessary if the director is fully to understand those clients for whom St Ignatius is the proper guide. Such an experience can even appear to be impious; playing around with prayer—our relationship with God in Christ—for an ulterior motive is not an ideal exercise. Yet it is the price spiritual directors have to pay for competent understanding of those different from themselves.

It is advisable to start by concentrating on one school at a time, over a fairly lengthy period, in order to grasp its theology, its taste, flavour, stress, and method. After some years the schools can be mixed up, in fact this is necessary if we are to keep abreast and fresh for the job. It is like the development of art appreciation. You begin with a pile of paintings, soon developing deeper insights into the various schools; Italian, Flemish, Renaissance, pre-Raphaelite, Impressionist and so on, until any example is easily classified at a glance. Further studies lead to greater expertise, so that clients whose prayer follows a school quite different from that of the director may be appreciated and not merely understood. In spite of all the necessary classification—the on-the-slab process—clients remain human beings with an integrated spirituality. A thorough appreciation of the individual schools, however diverse, cements this deep and creative relationship.

This study of ascetical theology is a properly objective exercise respecting the unique individuality of every client, and making allowance for the unique individuality of the director himself. But individuality implies community, and is nurtured by it: we are back to 1 Corinthians 12. Despite individuality, therefore, all Christians partake, to some extent, of a cultural and spiritual environment in which they live. Schools and their derivatives are frequently defined in terms of nationality: the Dominicans of the Rhineland (a little school very different from other aspects of Dominican spirituality), the Spanish Carmelites, the French Oratorians, and so on. The later schools, though founded upon

Scripture and the creeds, trace their ancestry to former schools from which they develop specially pronounced characteristics. So churches, sects, and denominations take on the qualities of a group of schools from which they have borrowed certain traits.

This underlying cultural-spiritual factor is always there, and when spirituality is strong and healthy it is prominent; we have to begin from where we are, so the ethos of a community or church has to be considered. There is an English spirituality (which I have tried to explain in a book of that name) and there is an Anglican spirituality. No good purpose is served—certainly not ecumenical interests—by pretending otherwise, for without the cultural background we have chaos. This cultural factor also helps to form a syllabus, or a timetable, for the study of the schools, thus simplifying things.

From an unashamedly Anglican viewpoint, therefore, or for that matter from a general western viewpoint, it is wise to begin with Benedictinism, based on the theology of St Augustine, for here is the root of the Western tradition. From there it is sensible to notice how Benedictinism developed into two inter-related but very different strains: Cluniac and Cistercian. It might then be sensible to go over to the other side and spend some time studying the Pseudo-Dionysian writings, especially noting the contrast. If we have accepted an Anglican starting point, not to be insular but to bring some order into things, we would move to St Anselm, still within the Benedictine stream but with notable characteristics all his own. Here I have suggested, is the patristic father of our own spiritual tradition, and the heart of the speculative–affective synthesis: the ultimate *via media*.

Then possibly a comparison between the friars, Dominican and Franciscan, and on perhaps to the fourteenth-century English school itself, the while sampling lesser movements, or those outside our specific make-up, on the way. Then through the Reformation period to the Caroline Divines, Protestant develop-ment, and the huge and ultimate corpus from Carmelite Spain.

This cultural factor is a little different from the influence of purely secular culture on prayer, since it is based upon spirituality itself, and yet the culture-or-fashion question still arises. There is, for example, a widespread movement from discursive meditation of the Ignatian type towards simple contemplative prayer. This is plainly of cultural significance since it grows out of the type of existentialist philosophy which seeks only to describe how modern people think and feel. On the other hand there is a growing interest in the western world in Eastern Orthodox ascetic, the cultural aspect of which is obscure: is this mere fashion? Certainly there are points of contact between East and West, the doctrine of creation being a major example, and yet it is hard to visualize anything like the Orthodox liturgy being absorbed into western-English spirituality, however inspiring it may be once in a while. Fashion or culture is an important question for the spiritual director to grapple with.

An example of these factors is the spiritual expression of Christians from the Xhosa tribe of the Republic of Transkei. Evangelized by the nineteenth-century British, notably by the Society of St John the Evangelist, the spirit of Western Christendom was planted onto a basically oriental and mystical race. The Xhosa rendering of the liturgy of the Book of Common Prayer, backed by well-worn Victorian hymnody, all in English, is the ultimate in ghastly dreariness. The same thing in the Xhosa language, accompanied by tribal folk-tunes, is as impressive and worshipful as the Orthodox liturgy: the one is an implanted fashion; the other a cultural adaptation. It seems a pity that Providence did not arrange for Southern African tribes to be evangelized by the Greeks or Russians! And it has been suggested that if and when the Africans give birth to a Christian school of prayer, then its twin emphases should be the doctrine of creation and the communion of saints.

The cultural factor further reminds us that tradition is a living, ever moving stream. It is as important for the spiritual director to read, study and pray with the great schools and guides from the past, as it is for him to take note of patristic and scholastic theology. But it is in the contemporary world that we work, and from which our clients come. The great schools of prayer also move and grow; the modern Benedictine is not the same as his forebears of Monte Cassino, and the French Cistercian is not the same as his American brother. It is as necessary to keep up with the trends in ascetical writing as it is to be aware of developments in biblical and theological studies.

This working partnership between the older and the newer theologies is especially relevant here, and exciting speculations arise. The modern radical will still claim that the classic expressions of Christian spirituality are based upon outmoded theological concepts, and are therefore to be discarded. It is certainly true that Benedictinism, old or new, is firmly rooted in the theology of St Augustine, with special reference to his trinitarian exposition. Precisely how does the Rule of St Benedict fare when confronted by existential doctrines of the Triune God? It is an absorbing question.

Chapter 12

Progression

So far we have been concerned with assessing what sort of a person, spiritually speaking, our client is; what are his gifts and failings, his temperamental bias, moral type and so on. But the Christian life of prayer is progressive, it cannot stand still, it must move and it must change.

Spiritual progress is embedded in the tradition; the move to what is technically and somewhat ambiguously called perfection, hence the host of classical titles that speak of journeys, scales, ladders and ways. Everyone does not take the same road; some progress by advancing in the type and technique of prayer itself, some by remaining on the same spiritual level and doing the same things better, some move in the direction of deeper intuitive insight, others move towards the prophetic, or to heightened spiritual experience.

Whatever the diversity, spiritual progress is subject to two initial and inviolable principles. The first is that the only valid test is moral theology: progress, whatever its exact nature, means committing less sin and growing more joyfully penitent. Secondly, the task of spiritual direction is to create and maintain spiritual health, on the assurance that growth will follow and that such growth will be according to the will of God for that person. The director is to aim at better prayer rather than different prayer; he is coach to a third-division team and his aim is to make it a better third-division team, and if it happens to get promoted into the second division then that is incidental. The classical progressions, therefore, are to be regarded as maps not itineraries; their initial piece of information is to tell you where you are. Then they can offer various routes towards your destination, but they are to be read with care and they are not in themselves routes.

Direction must, indeed, be able to discern changes in a client. It has to notice possible transference from one spiritual level to another, but it does not directly create the change: God alone can give the increase. The classical progressions need serious study, for they contain the wisdom of the ages, but they suffer from a certain archaism and they are still apt to be expounded within an equally archaic theological framework. They especially suffer from what has been described as the Pygmalion doctrine of man; the living statue image upon which a series of fixed characteristics are somehow attached. It is worth some attempt to update the traditional teaching.

The classical Three Ways—purgative, illuminative, unitive—or in its personal form—beginners, proficients, perfect—is the basis of them all, but, to say the least, the very words are somewhat off-putting! Purgation hints at the Pygmalion statue that has to be purged of sin as a fixed characteristic, as a kind of poison that has to be eradicated by some sort of spiritual laxative. Illumination, or intuition, or prophecy, sounds a little better because it moves away from the idea of a substance to an existential experience, while union with God is the ultimate aim.

In the personal form, 'beginner' sounds too precise to be true: a pristine Pygmalion statue. Here is a further warning against thinking too literally about climbing ladders and making journeys rather than about reading maps and consulting plans. Unitive saints, the perfect, are still sinners, while beginners are not wholly unillumined by grace: if they were they could not even begin.

The situation is not helped when comparatively modern writers—de Guibert, Bouyer, Häring—persist with the old substantive vocabulary. Qualities, virtues, gifts and graces, are still treated as substantial things to be acquired or infused. Yet the profound truth behind the classical teaching remains unimpaired. It needs reinterpreting so that it is more amenable to our clients, who are people; not living statues but existential beings.

The on-the-slab categories, although rooted in the ancient tradition, alleviate the problem, because they are not dependent upon cosy devotional idiom but upon ascetical theology. Speculative-affective, Arian-Apollinarian, Affirmation-Renunciation, immanent-transcendent; these are not substantial things, fixed characteristics of the soul-substance, but rather attitudes, existential tendencies, habits of outlook. Can the categories of progression be examined and brought more into line with this contemporary approach?

A beginner in the purgative way is too often presented as some special sort of animal who may one day metamorphose into something else, namely a proficient in the illuminative way. He is a particularly grimy sort of statue that wants a good wash before anything else. The beginner is not necessarily a vicious sinner to be purged, neither is he without gifts and graces; he is a flux of potentiality, and the most obvious thing about him is that his spiritual potential is unresolved by order and choice: he is in a muddle. His first need is for *regula*, system, to be worked out with the utmost care in accordance with *attrait*, remembering always that *regula*—Rule—is diametrically opposite to a list of little rules. It is unusual for a genuine *regula* to emerge after less than several sessions on the slab; clients should be warned not to expect too much too soon, and directors have to exercise patience before clear conclusions arise.

The actual prayer of beginners is usually a muddle precisely because he follows rules instead of Rule. His life is made up of little bits and pieces of intercession, self-examination, meditation, thanksgiving and so on, but with no reference to himself as person. By Rule the paradox of beloved Thomas and the fish on the slab is resolved. The first step in direction is most likely to find out precisely what our client is actually doing in terms of prayer and then cut half of it out. The need is for simplification, reducing chaos to order, integrating the potential, which is what the tradition means by recollection.

Recollective simplification is necessary because beginners usually fluctuate between enthusiasm and dejection—de Guibert speaks of indiscreet fervour—which is again because he is confronted with too many choices. This initial movement from spiritual chaos to integration is what tradition means by self-knowledge, the uncovering of *attrait*, which is where direction begins: what sort of fish is on the slab?

Responsible choice between possibilities, leading to the correct formulation of Rule, is the more positive equivalent to textbook self-examination; more positive because it is concerned with gifts as well as sins. The fight against sin continues for ever, and moral theology remains part and parcel of the simplification process— pride is not vanity and covetousness is not envy: these have to be clearly distinguished or we will be fighting with the wrong weapons. Yet in any context, the positive nurture of spiritual gifts is a potent weapon against sin in general: purgation is not a satisfactory word.

The directorial approach to beginners must certainly be concerned with the eradication of sin, and particularly with the recognition of its more subtle manifestation. It must also seek to unearth potential gifts and virtues, upon which tradition insists but which is too frequently overlooked: there is more in it than purgation. But this in no way overthrows tradition which, despite much pious verbosity and archaic terminology, ever insists upon the primacy of self-knowledge and self-acceptance. So it might help to translate beginners-in-the-purgative way by some such idea as clients in enthusiastic-panic; people in a muddle, or if the jargon is not too awful, those of unresolved spiritual potential.

The hallmark of proficiency—the illuminative way is here an even more misleading phrase—is stability, or maturity which has learned to ride lightly upon experience and consolation, not that experience is necessarily lacking but that it is accepted calmly and put into perspective. The proficient may not be far along the road but at least he has chosen a definite route and he knows where he is going, without bothering overmuch about the speed of his progress or the satisfactions of the scenery. Rule is embraced and also absorbed; it is part of life, spontaneous and without burden, issuing in habitual recollection.

Stability, however, is not a static state. It points to a vertical rather than to a horizontal movement; a deepening of faith which is also a heightening of love and loyalty. Proficiency is a good word, fully consonant with modern interpretation, but if we needed some equivalent to the enthusiastic-panic of beginners I would suggest something like arid-loyalty. The nuptial relation with God-in-Christ has moved from bubbly romance, with all of its muddled temperamental vicissitudes, to a deep and permanent loyalty: to descend to the jargon, commitment.

We are not here concerned with aridity in its acute and transitory form, which is always with everyone and common to all the Ways, but with that more chronic kind which is a sure sign of progress and common to any human endeavour. Sportsmen, writers, scholars, musicians, all eventually lose enthusiasm and get sick of the whole thing: it is part of the game. Chronic aridity is of particular importance to the director since it may well herald crisis periods, and therefore change, in a progressive development. Such crises confront the director with enormous difficulties of the most delicate kind: does the client need a rest, a holiday from the spiritual struggle, or should he plod on regardless? Is the crisis a normal process heralding change and advancement? And if so what sort of change is indicated? Or is the crisis due to the upsurge of sudden sin?

There can be no clear-cut answers, but the slab categories give solid hints. The speculative type may safely be persuaded to plod on; his affective brother probably needs a rest. The renunciative client is another natural plodder, well equipped to cope with the crisis, while the affirmative person could need some relaxation of Rule. The inclined-to-scrupulous must relax, even if he does not like it; the lax needs a modified plod, even if he finds it uncongenial. The categories, unearthed on the slab, remain only guidelines, pointers, but they are at least that.

If we are concerned with spiritual direction on a general-practitioner level, with pastoral ascetic rather than with mystical theology, little need be said about the perfect, or those in the unitive way. Few of our clients will be mystics in the full sense, although this does not rule out the possibility of genuine mystical experience of a transitory type. In any case these are the concern of the specialist consultant. Nevertheless to save some of the confusion arising out of this outmoded terminology it should be noticed that, like purgation and illumination, perfection is a technical archaism differing from its common meaning. First, it is a relative term denoting a way rather than a state, but a way that generally involves certain types of prayer and intrinsic moral characteristics. One can be imperfectly in the unitive way— imperfectly perfect. Conversely, to speak of God's absolute perfection is not to employ a superfluous adjective. Secondly, in a slightly different sense, perfection is a term applicable to anyone in any state; there can be perfect beginners and perfect proficients just as there can be perfect children and perfect adults. In its ascetical and mystical context the term really means complete conformity to the will of God, and God plainly wills that some remain in stage one all through life, ending up as perfect beginners. The director's concern, as team coach, is still to put his third-division club on top of the league table, not to push it up to the second division.

There is general consensus among the authorities, however, that the edges between the illuminative and unitive ways are very ragged indeed; that there is a kind of substantial no-man's-land dividing the two. In practice, few of our pastoral–parochial clients are likely to enter the mystical way of union, while not a few will move beyond proficiency. Pastoral ascetic demands an intermediate stage.

The term I would choose to assist modern spiritual directors is, with some modification, the traditional term: 'ligature'. Dr Trueman Dicken explains how this term was invented by Poulain, after a notion borrowed from Bossuet, elaborated and expanded by Dom John Chapman; and incidentally given added contemporary significance by Dr Trueman Dicken himself. For Dom John Chapman, the ligature is a convenient, pastorally orientated word, for the process that St John of the Cross calls the advent of the night of the senses. (Trueman Dicken, *The Crucible of Love*, pp. 163ff., 265-7, 288-91.)

'Ligature' means to tie up, but here it is used in the medical sense of strangulation, the cutting off of a haemorrhage. The night of the senses means their strangulation, so the term veers strongly towards the renunciative, *via negativa* type of spirituality that St John of the Cross largely embraces. The modern mood tends towards the affirmation of creation, giving rise to the common experience of a frustration, or cessation, of discursive thought. For contemporary direction the term we need could be ligature of the intellect, pointing to the stage when it becomes impossible to pray and think at the same time; a simple contemplative stance in which the senses, but not the intellect, play a proper and prominent part.

Dr Trueman Dicken's great book just cited was published in 1963, and it is interspersed with repetitive warnings to spiritual directors to look out for the ligature in their clients and then not to insist upon, but rather to dissuade from, discursive meditation. Discursive meditation is here regarded as the norm and foundation of ordinary prayer, and it is questionable whether this assumption still pertains: again we confront changing cultural patterns.

It depends upon *attrait*, but generally speaking, the direction of proficients in 1963 was based on the 1-2-3, a-b-c type of discursive meditation, and most clients took it up with excited enthusiasm.

The majority of today's clientele are bored stiff with it at any stage. The reasons for the change are cultural and subtle, and they have been explained and analysed many times. And I am certainly not questioning the important warnings offered by Dr Trueman Dicken. The contemporary issue is that, whereas the ligature of the intellect heralded a comparatively advanced state twenty years ago, it is now a much more frequent experience which arises considerably earlier.

Contemplation used to be a frightening word, and it is one which comprehends a vast range of prayer and experience. But if its root meaning indicates an integrated, intuitive, experiential approach to prayer instead of a discursive intellectual one, then it has now become the norm. *Mandala* experiments of contemplating a crucifix or a flower, or of absorbing the Holy Trinity through the contemplation of a triangular symbol, do not imply advanced states of spiritual perception, but they are generically contemplative and not intellectual. Such popular spiritual exercises lead easily into contemplation of the mystery of the Holy Trinity interpreted as Triune Being, rather than to discursive consideration upon (a) Father, (b) Son, (c) Spirit. Father, Son and Spirit remain in the director's head, Triune Being in his client's heart. *Mantra* prayer, such as the Jesus prayer of Orthodoxy, also gains steadily in popularity, expressing the same cultural movement away from discursive intellection towards contemplative simplicity.

Such cultural patterns and changes have to be considered, especially since, without defying tradition, they are apt to abrogate certain customary presuppositions. This pertains to prayer types commonly supposed to be intrinsic to the Ways: that which is at the very heart of direction. For example—and somewhat to simplify—it is supposed that thoughtful vocal prayer is right for beginners in the purgative way; that discursive meditation is the heart of proficiency; and that any sort of contemplation is the prerogative of the perfect. Allowing for necessary blurred edges such a scheme can no longer be assumed: the simple contemplation of a clover leaf might do more for a modern beginner than instruction in trinitarian doctrine, especially if he veers to the affective side.

Intellect is part of the human make-up which is not to be discounted and can never be eliminated, but emphases change with cultural patterns. Exaggeration of intellection has ever been an Anglican failing; faith and reason interact but they are never synonyms. To the eighteenth century reason was all, but the modern pendulum has swung far from that position, and not unhealthily.

Meanwhile, back to the slab.

The tradition has to be studied and where possible updated, which means a good deal of examination of ambiguous terminology. That in itself is no new thing: St Teresa of Avila admitted confusion as to what illumination meant and plainly disliked the term. Neither can the traditional words be changed, because the student of ascetical theology will come across them and must come to terms with them. This may complicate our studies but it does not matter very much since the technical terms themselves need play no part in direction: we have to know that our client is a world-affirming Apollinarian in the illuminative way, but there is no need to tell him quite like that. The important thing is our approach, combining the ancient wisdom of tradition with both contemporary theological expression and cultural factors pertaining to age and place.

So our beginner-client is not, as a superficial study of the text-book might suggest, simply a vicious sinner to be purged: a filthy soul-substance statue with which nothing can be done until its cracks have been remedied and it has had a good scrub with carbolic soap. Neither is he—before or after such treatment—*tabula rasa*, a nice clean lump of clay to be moulded into his director's own beautiful image. He is Thomas, a beloved brother in Christ, to be loved and cherished within the sacred humanity, a vital participant in the local Body of Christ. But the only way to express this sort of quite genuine gush is to slap him on the slab; rather than cold impersonal clinicism this is the way of expressing our concern for Thomas's human dignity. Confronted with a beginner, which we take to imply an initial interview, the modern director looks for potential; first God's gifts, second the sins which are frustrating them. And he expects a muddle, he expects to have to sort things out, he expects an enthusiasm-aridity, 'this prayer-that prayer' conflict, but underneath is potential Saint Thomas.

There is more than one route to one's final destination; the windy old country lane or the motorway—affective or speculative

—the one pretty, emotive, and subjectively stimulating; the other fast, direct, tough and proficient. You can walk, run, drive, fly or catch a train. The important thing is to discover what is best for Thomas, and having done this from the slab, rigorously cut out all the alternatives. The process leads into self-knowledge of the classical tradition, but it clothes it with ascetical as well as moral and psychological elements. Gifts, graces, *attrait* are as much part of a client's nature as the other elements, and nature is to be perfected by grace.

The proficiency stage is at the heart of the directorial process, which is not amenable to slick guidelines. Having initiated the basic *regula*-pattern there must be constant vigil for subtle changes, new temptations, fresh experiences, or fresh absences of experience. This is the heart of the matter. In context, suffice it to point to the error and ambiguity implied in the classical phrase, 'the Illuminative Way'; and this with St Teresa's support. Truly, at this stage, illumination, or better, intuition, may play a part, while we look, primarily, not for these characteristics but for stability; for maturity, for ability to cope, for habitual recollection, and for unfussy moral growth.

The critics of traditional ascetic, accusing it of verbal archaism, of outmoded theology, and of artificial complexity, have a case, but clarity emerges from a return to the biblical basis as outlined in chapter 8, section 2. The purgative, illuminative, unitive ways—equalling beginners, proficients and perfect—make more practical, directorial sense when we return to the three-fold biblical relationship: covenant, encounter, incorporation.

The first point about this biblical progression is that although it is a progression, showing how prayer-relationship between man and God moves from the remote to the intimate, it avoids the dangers of regarding spiritual life as a neat series of stages; the danger inherent in the scales, ladders and journeys. The biblical progression is one of emphasis rather than clear-cut phases. Covenant implies obedience to divine law enacted by a transcendent God, and this relation ever pertains to all Christians, be they beginners or saints. On the other hand the Christian is always 'in Christ', incorporated into the sacred humanity by baptism, and therefore in a real sense in union with God. Prayer always includes the element of encounter: the nuptial analogy again, wherein the twain are one flesh while remaining two individuals. All three stages are summed up in the eucharistic prayer: 'This is my blood of the new covenant . . . do this . . .' For here is covenant, demanding obedience, encounter, the sacramental presence, and incorporation or communion.

The prayer proper to each stage, as emphasis not exclusion, is also clarified without going against the tradition. Covenant stresses obedience to given law, the transcendence, or otherness, or remoteness, of God Almighty. Prayer then will include a large element of penitence, and this will be supported by the moral struggle: purgation. The classic tradition suggests that prayer at this stage is largely vocal, discursive, and educative; the divine commands, or God's side of the covenant, need to be studied and understood. At this stage *regula* has to emerge, both in accordance with theology and with personal *attrait*, but with the emphasis on transcendence the divine office plays a vital part. *Regula* becomes the Christian way of both obedience to law and response to love: the biblical progression eliminates any conflict between law and gospel.

From the Christian standpoint, the new covenant sees Jesus primarily as teacher, mediator, and intercessor. The New Testament ethic has to be absorbed and understood, either by biblical studies or by discursive meditation of some kind. Special attention is to be paid to our Lord's actual teaching about prayer with particular attention to the analysis and interpretation of the *Pater Noster*.

This first stage leads naturally into the second, from Covenant to Encounter, because encounter with the living and glorified Lord implies some kind of discursive meditation on the Gospel narrative. Jesus is seen first as covenant authority, secondly as living presence. We are at the discursive, intellectual stage, far from the ligature, but the cultural factor which runs counter to discursive meditation must be taken into account. Meditation need not be of the rigid, quasi-Ignatian type, and contemporary Christians may well pass through this phase fairly rapidly. Emphasis on personal integration, on potentiality rather than substantive qualities, on total experience instead of pure cognition has led thousands of the modern faithful to simple non-discursive prayer: the encounter of the whole man with the whole Christ. Such prayer has to be called contemplative, although there is nothing very special or advanced about it.

A further advantage of the biblical scheme and terminology is that stage three—incorporation—makes pastoral sense, whereas the perfect-in-the-unitive way approach is liable to get lost in the quasi-mystical clouds. By baptism and Holy Communion the Christian is in union with God in Christ, sin and frailty notwithstanding. That is no pious hope, no personal ascetical achievement, but a theological fact. To be one with Christ, wedded to Christ, whereby the whole person, senses, appetites, emotions, intellect and the rest, partake of all aspects of the sacred humanity, is nothing extraordinary but the Christian status. Yet it is remarkable, in the face of St Paul, how little is made of this theology in spiritual direction and in its impingement on ordinary contemplative prayer.

None of this is to deny that true mystical union is something special which is unlikely to impinge upon spiritual direction on a pastoral level. But it is misleading to deny by implication that all of humanity and the whole creation is in some sense in union with God, for that would imply a general annihilation.

The spiritual director is expected to have absorbed the teaching of the biblical and classical progressions, difficult and ambiguous as this may be. Can it be further simplified, brought more into line with pastoral experience? In chapter 5 I attempted to explain the fundamental love-on-the-slab categories as expressed in classical ascetic. And I followed this examination, in chapter 6, with some speculation as to how this could be simplified and brought up to date in the contemporary pastoral setting. Can the same process be applied to the traditional idea of progression? It might be worth a try.

Chapter 13

Progression: Ancient and Modern

THE SPIRITUAL DIRECTOR awaits his client, unknown or known by passing acquaintance. He, the director, is armed with his professional learning, with the on-the-slab ascetical categories, and with the theology of progression; he has absorbed the sound, detailed, authoritative, and infuriating complexity and ambiguity of the three-ways system. He knows that this is essential, yet he has rationalized it, or tried to, by reference back to its biblical foundation. As primarily a pastor–director rather than an ascetical theologian—although it should be plain by now that you cannot be the one without the other—what does he expect of his client?

The first and obvious answer is nothing: preconceived notions are disastrous. Direction has to start with an objective blank. Yet certain expectations are reasonable, and the textbooks support them. The classic tradition is aimed initially at monastic order and latterly at the devout minority: from St Benedict to St François de Sales. So the terminology of the textbook again lets us down; beginners-in-the-purgative way are not quite what that phrase sounds like. Let it be remembered that direction, in the modern pastoral sense, embraces seven-year-old confirmands and illiterates, as well as reasonably intelligent and advanced people. But by and large our clients are going to be of the latter type. In directorial terms they are beginners because they are about to begin, seriously, but they will have had a good deal of trial and error experience, which is why the first job is to eliminate the error; to cut out three-quarters of their present prayer experiment and reduce the chaos to something like order. They are not beginners in the sense of someone who decides to take up golf having never swung a club before. They will be sinners—are not we all?—but not necessarily in the fundamental state of purgation where resistance to temptation

105

is the most obvious starting point. There will be gifts and graces to discover, *regula* either to initiate or to confirm, or more likely to simplify and rationalize. Let us then attempt to simplify the tradition in more pastoral terms.

1. The three-ways system obviously looks to the Eucharist as central to Christian life, but this is not too clearly spelled out. The spirituality of the early Christian centuries, certainly to the time of the Pseudo-Dionysius and largely up to St Bernard, was strongly liturgical, centred upon the Benedictine-Cluniac tradition. Later spirituality became more personal and a good deal of medieval ascetic appears, at first sight, to divorce personal prayer from liturgy. No such error is risked once we return to the biblical categories, for covenant-encounter-incorporation is pregnant with eucharistic associations. Since the Eucharist is where any beginner has to begin, the progression based upon it might be pastorally useful. Such a progression could be expressed as covenant-obedience, encounter-presence, incorporation-adoration. This is worthy of further examination.

The beginner's initial response must be simple obedience to the covenant command: do this in remembrance of me. Next comes the attempt to grasp the significance of eucharistic doctrine, to follow the liturgical structure and meditate upon its meaning. This will imply preparation by self-examination, penitence, confession and forgiveness: in other words purgation. These emphases will always play some part, though varying according to *attrait*, but they will proportionally diminish as one grows into wider implications of eucharistic worship.

The common criticism of Anglican liturgy is that it over-stresses subjectivism and penitence. Important as those aspects are, they do not constitute the whole of eucharistic worship. Faith in the Real Presence, however interpreted, means encounter with the risen and glorified Lord; thanksgiving for the redemption of the whole created universe enters in. The Eucharist takes on a cosmic significance as it moves from a discursive series of prayers towards an integrated act. Penitential prayer, historical event, the message of the lections, subjective and objective emphases, still remain but they move towards a synthetic act. Books, commentaries, lections, so necessary at the covenant stage, now tend to become at best superfluous and at worst a positive hindrance. The custom whereby all entering a church are offered a battery of books by a beaming churchwarden is a little disturbing, pointing to the tacit assumption that all Anglicans are condemned for ever to the beginner state.

At this stage of encounter-proficiency what may properly be called a contemplative, or non-discursive approach will sometimes lead into genuine experience of the present Lord, of succour, acceptance, forgiveness and grace: that could be called illumination but the term is still misleading.

Holy Communion and incorporation mean practically the same thing, and the incorporative experience could be called unitive, yet the time-honoured term still does not quite fit. This is the final pastoral stage in which, incorporated into the sacred humanity, partaking of the sacramental, life-giving blood, being in-Christ, it is possible with the aid of the Spirit to adore the Blessed Trinity. That is the ultimate consummation of eucharistic worship and it is not inconsistent with penitence, or cognition, or theological understanding.

Such a eucharistic progression follows the traditional pattern, but it is simpler, more directly pastoral, and of more obvious directorial use. To find out how a client approaches the Eucharist, what it really means to him, what sort of experience—if any—he associates with it, is not a bad way to conduct an initiatory interview with a reticent client. It gives more than a clue to his status according to the three-ways pattern and may well unearth his fundamental slab-classification.

2. Another pastoral progression might be described as morality-liturgy-prayer, or as a variation, evangelism-ecclesiasticism prayer. The Christian ethic, involving purgation of sin as its prerequisite, is often the beginner's main interest and inspiration. It is expressed either in practical service to others or in evangelistic witness, often with Pelagian overtones. It is the enthusiasm of the beginner in any context: to share one's new-found enthusiasm; to get involved in the institutional ethos of that enthusiasm, be it church, committee, or golf club; and only finally to get down to the solid business of what the enthusiasm is all about.

Moral progress in terms of practical service to others is an admirable ideal, until it is realized that without grace it becomes both unbearable and impossible; hence the later preoccupation with liturgy, or with ecclesiastical bureaucracy as a busy second-best. Then you start playing the real game: prayer.

This pastoral progression might be simplified further: people-ecclesiasticism-God. Out of twenty average candidates for ordination, nineteen start by wanting to serve their neighbours, and to some extent they are all tarred with the ecclesiastical brush. One out of twenty—if you are lucky—seeks the priesthood because he wants to serve God. (At a recent conference for potential ordinands there was lively and knowledgeable discussion on various 'counselling' problems: marital, emotional, financial, medical and moral. When I asked what was the pastoral approach to the faithful, who had not got any hang-ups, there was blank surprise and stony silence: the epitome of the ambulance syndrome.)

The desire for personal moral improvement, coupled with practical service to others, is neither specifically Christian nor religious. Ecclesiasticism, whether expressed by preoccupation with liturgy or with bureaucracy, is a curious contagion: it can get you badly. But these are legitimate stages on the way to prayer, to proficiency, and they should be accepted as such. Only by careful, patient guidance, can these preliminary stages be lived through and made creative by their final supercession by prayer; that is by a living and continuous relation with God in Christ. It is still a question of covenant-encounter-incorporation, and it is still assumed that, although legitimate stages, all these aspects continue to play their part in the final proficient synthesis. Concern for others, enthusiasm for the practical affairs of the local church, and liturgical enthusiasm, need never vanish. It is a question of proportion, balance and proficient synthesis.

There is a final, composite progression which is also not found in the classic texts, but which summarizes all the others and which I think remains consonant with the tradition: God-the-Provider, God-the-Lover, God-the-Disturber. Initially God is seen as loving and helpful, present in human life, solving problems, a very present help in trouble: the ambulance syndrome. Once the beginner gets over this stage penitence arises; we are in trouble because we deserve to be but God still provides in the form of forgiveness. Crudely he is there to come to our aid, to be subjectively useful. All of which has obvious associations with the purgative way, or with the way of the covenant relation.

As love supplants usefulness the proficient stage is entered, and the love of God progresses throughout this second phase: from romanticism to loyalty, despite aridities and desolation. And this, too, has obvious connections with the notion of Christ-encounter. It is predominantly through Jesus that the love of God is expressed to men, and it is through him that illumination comes into experience.

Somewhere in the proficient stage God appears as awkward, as demanding, as the disturber of ordinary aspirations and values: the all-holy transcendence. Finally God is God. That is perfection and there is no more to be said, let alone thought. In quite normal experience we are at the ligature stage: God is God. In terms of prayer we have moved from petition to penitence to adoration, from the subjective to the objective.

All progressions are ultimately trinitarian formulae: the doctrine of the Trinity must never leave the director's mind, but progressions usually pose the doctrine the wrong way round, that is the unconventional way round. The modern charismatic movement is an obvious example, for it starts with experience of the Holy Spirit, the subjective comforter, the helper and inspirer. The so-called baptism of the Spirit, the twice-born experience, is typical of the beginner; oscillating experience, uncontrolled fervour, and artless enthusiasm. Encounter, relation with the living Lord, soon enters, but it is still subjective, this-worldly but without any necessary affirmation of creation. None of this is adversely critical, for it is a valid starting point, but proficiency only enters with the transcendent dimension of the majestic Father in glory: adoration is the ultimate end.

Such modern-pastoral progressions, useful as they may be to the director, have no authority whatever, except in so far as they are reducible to facets of the classical tradition. I suggest, for example, that the progression just examined—Provider-Lover-Disturber— is closely akin to the *De Diligendo Deo* of St Bernard of Clairvaux, but, with respect, in an idiom that makes this supreme teaching more usable in the twentieth century. It is surely in line with St Bernard's underlying counsel: discover where one's client *is* (the slab-process); never mind where you think he ought to be, because under the divine providence where he ought to be is where he is. From the slab look ahead, but not too far ahead.

There is still no substitute for personal absorption of the

classical tradition, for first-hand acquaintance with the masters: St Augustine, St Anselm, St Bernard, St Teresa; with the Dominicans and the Franciscans; with Bossuet and Scaramelli; with Jeremy Taylor and Robert Sanderson; with contemporary writers on the subject; and indeed with others concerned with subsidiary disciplines which may shed light on the quest for a contemporary under-standing of the ancient wisdom. The time has come for a preliminary skirmish into one such subsidiary discipline.

Chapter 14

Socio-Theology: A Curious Courtship

ALL TOO frequently studies in religious psychology are either grossly heretical (if one takes the orthodox line) or they repeat the wisdom of orthodoxy but in a different jargon. The latter kind have value in that they can illuminate tradition as well as substantiating it in the minds of modern people.

One such book is Bruce Reed's *The Dynamics of Religion* (published by Darton, Longman and Todd in 1978), which could prove to be an intriguing companion for the modern spiritual director. It carries the sub-title *Process and Movement in Christian Churches*, and it is written from the social psychological stand-point, quite correctly discarding theological presuppositions except for an occasional illustration.

The first problem is to try to translate the terminology (one is sorely tempted to say jargon) and to try to relate this to the terms of ascetical theology (which in fairness can equally be called jargon). The fundamental thesis is called the 'oscillation theory' which follows the dictionary definition: 'oscillation' is to swing like a pendulum; to move to and fro between two points. Here it refers to oscillation between two alternating modes of thought, or outlook, or experience. These two alternating modes or poles are variously described, the basic distinction being that between 'religious' and 'secular' activity.

A further distinction is that between 'process' and 'movement'. The former asks the question: why do people alternate between everyday life and religious services? And further: what actually happens at such services, from a behavioural or psychological viewpoint? The latter is the attempt to offer a rationale of such behaviour, that is, from a quasi-theological viewpoint.

The thesis is concerned with the psychological concept of dependence, of which there are again two kinds: 'extra-dependence' implies dependence upon someone or something outside oneself, a protector or sustainer, an external support. 'Intra-dependence' means self-dependence or self-reliance: the two 'oscillate'.

The last two polarities in this initial discussion (there are plenty more to come) concern psychological activity: 'S-activity' means, if I have grasped the meaning, Symbolism (S) which implies intuition, artistic creation, creative bi-sociation (to use Arthur Koestler's term), and ultimately, the cultus, ritual, emotion, and contemplative prayer. 'W-activity' means everyday rationalism (W equals work). So W-activity means the ordinary practical application to everyday reality.

According to Reed, none of these polarities should be classified as right or wrong. 'Oscillation' means that both poles enter into a normal and healthy life, religious or otherwise, and that health—social, individual, religious, or spiritual—means coming to terms with the interactions and balances between these various polarities: 'oscillation'.

Having tried to explain the terminology as best I can—recognizing the fact that anyone seriously interested must read and re-read *The Dynamics of Religion* for himself—we might pause to consider what all this new-fangled science has got to do with the spiritual direction of the faithful by those who claim to be qualified so to do, and so qualified by the orthodox tradition. There are many points of meeting.

First, 'oscillation'. The Fathers, from Tertullian and Origen onwards, accept precisely the same kind of process. They call it by various names, notably 'periodicy', but I think they refer to Bruce Reed's category: individuals have pendulum-type cycles, called in the classic tradition, 'consolation' and 'desolation'; 'aridity' and 'illumination'; in Old Testament terms, the prayer of the wild, desolate mountain top to the prayer of the worldly plain; from the desert—the *eremos* of silence to the market place— from 'S-activity to W-activity', from 'extra-dependence to intra-dependence'. Is there nothing new under the sun?

But yes, I think there is. The Fathers spoke in terms of Reed's 'process'—this is what happens. Reed goes on to 'movement' which explains why it happens, and so helps the spiritual director enormously. We are back to the ascetical progressions. Bruce Reed attacks the Bunyan *Pilgrim's Progress* sort of progression as a nice gentle upward movement, the classical ladder, scale, journey, and I have already given warning against this misinterpretation in chapter 12. But correctly interpreted, the Fathers of the Church are all on Reed's side (or is he on theirs?). The gentle progression idea is nowhere in the tradition: 'oscillation–periodicity' is everywhere in the tradition. Neither is tradition confined to 'oscillation' between religious categories. Indeed it is concerned with the 'oscillation' or 'periodicy' between consolation and desolation in prayer, between the meditative and the contemplative (allied with intra-dependence–extra-dependence—W-activity-S-activity), but also with what Reed insists upon: that 'oscillation' is concerned not only within religion, but as a polarity between religion and worldly life.

Secondly, dependence is a key word which has much to say about spiritual direction. Intra-dependence and extra-dependence alternate in a healthy life, neither can be called right or wrong, good or bad, but it is the oscillation process itself, or what Reed calls 'regression' from one to the other, which makes for sanity and balance. The directorial relationship implies a client who is extra-dependent upon his director to whom he goes for encouragement, guidance and support. But the healthy directorial interview aims at achieving regression to intra-dependence; the client has to stand on his own feet nurturing his own *attrait* and finding his own way. Too much reliance on the director—extra-dependence—is the wrong sort of paternalism; the attempt to make one's own way without direction at all—intra-dependence—is vanity, or undue self-reliance. The idea of regression from one to the other describes the healthy and creative relationship very well.

In Reed's terminology the ascetical slab could be coupled with the 'process', for it is the initial examination of what happens, what the client is like. But direction leads into the 'movement', the rationale or interpretation of the slab categories.

The extra-dependent mode means a reliance upon symbol and cultus, a quest for support from something or someone outside oneself. Regression to intra-dependence implies a self-reliance which can get on without such symbolic support. This seems to enlighten the distinction I have made between 'amateur' and 'professional' *attrait*. The latter is the client who enthuses over elaborate ritual, haunts the church building, and surrounds himself with ecclesiastical pictures, icons and statues. The former is one whose prayer does not depend on such symbols, to whom a cabbage, or nothing, is as good as a crucifix.

This is enlightening, because in practical life the amateur will regress to the extra-dependent mode by entering into liturgical worship and seeking direction, then to regress to his intra-dependent *attrait*. The professional, on the other hand, is in danger of failing to make such regression to the intra-dependent mode; in plain language to get unhealthily stuck in the ecclesiastical rut. Perceptive confirmation candidates sometimes ask what happens when a group of faithful laity get stranded on a desert island without Bibles, prayer-books, priests, patens and chalices. The answer is that professionals find themselves in a sorry state while amateurs manage perfectly well, making regression to the intra-dependent mode.

A similar argument applies to the more orthodox distinction between world-affirmation and world-renunciation, or between spirituality which is incarnational and sacramental on the one hand and of the mystical, *via negativa* type on the other. The first is extra-dependent on external symbols, be they crucifixes or cabbages; the second tries to do without them.

What is especially illuminating is that, while it has been insisted that *attrait* is to be nurtured, part of such nurture is that it should occasionally be curbed: the natural world-affirmer needs mortification while, carried to its logical conclusion, *via negativa* mysticism ceases to be incarnational. Saints of this tradition have been known to reject the sacraments: intra-dependence gone slightly mad. Spiritual health is neither the one nor the other but oscillation between the two; regression from one to the other.

While these categories—amateur-professional and affirmation-renunciation—are valid on-the-slab distinctions, should they not be seen also as progressions; as properly alternating phases of the spiritual life? A further curious result issues from this examination. If Bruce Reed's thesis may be adapted in this way, then, as criterion of spiritual health, the amateur comes off better than the professional because his life alternates between extra-dependence on liturgical symbol—S-activity—and creative life in the world—W-activity. Similarly world-affirmation, interspersed with necessary exercises in mortification, appears healthier than the thorough-going *attrait* towards world-renunciation, irrespective of the incarnational problems associated with this stance.

Thirdly, a curious yet exciting interchange arises between modern social psychological and ancient ascetical theology. Bruce

Reed illustrates his oscillation, extra-dependence–intra-dependence theory, by observing the relation between a two-year-old child and his mother:

> Not long ago I saw this scene in the Public Garden in Boston. The mothers were chatting on a bench while the children roamed around. For a while they would explore boldly and freely, ignoring their mothers. Then, after a while, they would use up their store of courage and confidence, and run back to their mothers' sides, and cling there for a while, as if to recharge their batteries. After a moment or two of this stay they were ready for more exploration, and so they went out, then came back, and then ventured out again. (p.13)

Now the extraordinary thing about this is that the oscillation theory, with its curious social-psychological terminology, introduces an idiom which could only make sense in the twentieth century. Yet it substantiates the same principles which underlie the Benedictine *Regula*, which in turn is dismissed by modern radical theology as hopelessly archaic. If scorn is poured on an outmoded 'God-in-the-gaps' then Bruce Reed would appear to be all in favour of him; if the divine office, the Benedictine *opus Dei*, is pietism based on an obsolete theology, then twentieth-century social psychology thinks otherwise.

The respective terminologies—or jargons—are practically parallel. Thus the Benedictine *Rule* looks like the process while Benedictine life is the movement; the extra-dependent mode is expressed by *opus Dei*, office and liturgy, while the intra-dependent mode is the Benedictine life in community. S-activity is parallel with *opus Dei*, W-activity is what Benedictinism is all about: work. Extra-dependence–intra-dependence—S-activity–W-activity could very well be translated by actual and habitual recollection.

There is one small snag. Curiously Reed, the ultra-twentieth-century sociologist, is out of date in a way that St Benedict is not, because he makes a clear distinction between religion—the cultus—and the rest of life. Benedictinism carefully avoids this error, the wrong sort of God-in-the-gaps distinction against which moderns like Kierkegaard and Bonhoeffer rightly rebelled.

To be extra-dependent on God is humility; intra-dependence is its proper outcome, but only when absolute dependence is internalized and held subconsciously. In ascetical terms, actual recollection leads into habitual recollection: conscious attention upon God in prayer and cult leads to subconscious reliance on God in humility. Christians can never become *in*dependent of God—the main strength of Schleiermacher.

Incarnational prayer is founded in baptism; it is the given and unbreakable relation with God in Christ through incorporation into the sacred humanity. So there might be subconscious-humility-intra-dependence but there can be no gaps. Acts of prayer, devotion and the cultus, are concentrates of a total relationship: Christian S-activity is a concentrate of W-activity. The ultimate oscillation is not between religion and life but between conscious attention to God and subconscious reliance upon him.

Bruce Reed might challenge this interpretive criticism, which in any case is an intrusion of theology into an admittedly non-theological study. The discussion is useful for spiritual direction, since modern sociological science enlightens and supports traditional ascetic, which nevertheless may move more deeply beyond it. The ideas behind extra-intra-dependence, S–W-activity, are familiar to St Benedict, even if the terminology is not.

Fourthly, Part II of *The Dynamics of Religion* gets down to pastoral and parochial brass tacks as it treats of the work and function of the local church in relation to the environment in which it is set. We are introduced to still more jargon: 'Process' and 'Movement' are translated as the Church's *manifest* function and its *latent* function. The first means something like the liturgical cultus—what the Church does; the second is its subtler, long-term influence on the surrounding environment. The relation is illustrated by an analogy to bees (p.145):

> If bees could talk, and we came across them busy in a flower garden and enquired what they were doing, their reply might be: 'Gathering nectar to make honey.' But if we asked the gardener, he would almost certainly answer: 'They are cross-pollinating my flowers.' In carrying out their manifest function to make food, the bees were performing a latent function of fertilising flowers. The mutual dependence of bees and flowers is an analogue of churches and society.

From this thesis, elaborated by Reed throughout chapter 7, several points of interest to our own arguments arise.

1. There is an initial pointer to that cultural factor which always impinges upon ascetical theology. The manifest function of the Church is prayer, worship, liturgy, preaching and so on, or if you like, and as Reed likes enormously, 'healthy regression to extra-dependence'. That is an acknowledgement of dependence upon God, expressed by cultic symbol, leading through humility to worship. The Church's latent function is what theology has always maintained it to be: evangelism, in its true and deep sense, conversion, the unleashing of spiritual power upon the world and ultimately the redemption of all creation.

2. Functional religion, the creative kind, is that which both co-operates with and yet challenges the wider cultural environment. Dysfunctional religion, or the sterile sort, is that which is only concerned with its own survival, inbred pietism, or in Reed's phrase 'a private club looking for subscribers'. Give me my honey, never mind the flowers. So the Church, that is, its locally committed members or regular congregation, is always of vicarious significance. Healthy participation in prayer or liturgy, whether magnificently corporate or privately hidden away, is always representative; on behalf of others, of concern with the environment.

3. The efficacy of the liturgy, that is, the move from manifest to latent function, or from the honey to the flowers, depends on the depth and purity of the faith of each individual member of the local Body. The ultimate need for functional, or creative, religion must be competent spiritual direction.

4. The essential pastoral (and sociological) need is not the modernization or simplification of liturgy, but the enabling of worshippers to comprehend the language of Christian symbolism; that is, to be under direction.

> The clarification of Elizabethan terminology in Bible and Prayer Book is laudable, but the mystery and vitality of worship can be easily dissipated in the name of simplification. The promotion of 'instant worship' to make services attractive to the unchurched and to children has the effect of denying the struggle to come face to face with God . . . The essence of the liturgy is that it is not 'new' but 'renewed'. Its purpose is to rehearse a given symbolic language which resonates with the surrounding culture. (p. 150)

117

Similarly preaching, as part of liturgy, should be directed at expounding the classical symbolism. It should be more theological than topical:

> Therefore sermons which direct attention to social and political issues would be usually more effective delivered from public platforms than from pulpits. (p.153)

On p.148 Reed illustrates this with the inevitable yet illuminating diagram, The Church's task can be put into socio-logical terms and translated back into theology to the support and enlightenment of both. By going to Church Christians regress to the extra-dependent mode; they comprehend more and more deeply the Christian symbolism associated with the worship of God. Then they healthily regress to intra-dependence, standing on their own feet in their own faith.

In humility dependence on God is recognized. Prayer and worship within liturgical action issues in mission, either directly or otherwise: the manifest function leads into the latent function. It is to be hoped that the same process, or the beginnings of it, would apply to occasional attendance by an honest enquirer. But that happy conclusion depends entirely on the proper functioning of the liturgical congregation, which depends in turn upon the competent spiritual direction of each individual within it. 'A happy welcome to this nice simple service' is *not* supported by religious sociology; 'Take up thy cross and follow me' *is*. Meanwhile the essential affirmation–renunciation conflict, with its vicarious and inter-cessory elements remains.

According to Reed there are four forms of Christian ministry whose function and inter-relation is illustrated by a diagram on p.170. These are priest, pastor, evangelist and prophet, which may be seen either as specific vocations or combined as aspects of the work of the same person. This latter option is unideal because all have their respective roles to play in the total oscillation process, and disastrous confusion may result when one person attempts to undertake them all. Reed, in other words, pinpoints the notorious Anglican difficulty whereby the single-handed parish priest is forced to try to be too many things at once. His thesis supports team ministries as well as the plea for an emphasis on priesthood as against the multifarious tangential duties which have become attached to the parson's role; in other words a return to true professionalism.

At first sight, and from my own theological standpoint, Reed's conception of priesthood is horrifying. On the surface he, the priest, appears as some sort of sacerdotal play-actor, a manipulator of persons and congregations according to socio-psychological techniques. Yet, when he is properly permitted his chosen context, valuable and orthodox conclusions emerge.

> The role of the priest is:
> to ensure the performance of the primary task of the local church by setting up activities which contain or render manageable the anxieties associated with the profane world. (p.169)

That looks horribly like the ambulance syndrome until it is recognized that the core of this process is regression to extra-dependence, or the liturgical expression of trust in God.

To continue, the priest

> does this through the following three sub-tasks:
> (a) to assist worshippers and prospective worshippers to manage their regression to extra-dependence;
> (b) to provide opportunities for them to worship God;
> (c) to provide opportunities for them to make the transition from extra-dependence to intra-dependence.

Simply translated the need is for spiritual direction: (a) means training in and preparation for liturgical worship; (b) and (c) are the aspect of spiritual direction which stresses habitual recollection in life, which guards against the dangers of pious introspection, and which sees prayer as a positive contribution to the redemption of the world.

So this scientific sociological study comes down heavily in favour of the priest as *sacerdos*. The function of the Church is *worship*, the priestly function is set within the sanctuary: '. . . the priest role of clergy relates the ministry to the sacred space . . .' (p.181).

The other three functionaries fit around this centrality of prayer and worship. The pastor's job is to prepare for this central activity, mainly through 'advising, counselling, teaching . . .'

(p.181). The evangelist is 'to make available the symbolic language of the Christian movement as an interpretation of the oscillation process' (p.184). In other words he is to preach the gospel, and according to Reed very much the whole gospel. This could be a large part of the Church's latent function, fertilizing the flowers, but it is absolutely dependent on the manifest function.

> By temperament evangelists may therefore be classed as fighters and flighters, and often they have few scruples in turning the Gospel into slogans—'Ye must be born again'. Local churches which focus attention on evangelism instead of grappling with the issues of dependence in depth take this for granted. For them the need is to arm the 'christian soldiers' for the fight, and worship as we have expounded it is neglected. (p.185)

Simply translated again, evangelism without prayer is sterile. Reed's prophet role follows the Old Testament tradition:

> The task of the prophet is to evaluate the performance by the church of its primary task. He does not judge its effectiveness by its attendance, spirituality, or the scope of its activities, which are the measures so often used by the members of the churches themselves. His yardstick is the state of the society in which the church works. (p.187)

Following tradition, Reed's brief description of the prophet is an inspiring passage, with a healthy stress on the need for the church's constant, corporate self-examination. We are reminded of Fr Christopher Wansey's *The Clockwork Church*: 'When the Church goes like clockwork, it is time for her to examine her inner life, and to seek to re-form its outward expression.'

The most curious thing of all is that here and throughout the whole book, Bruce Reed is making the strongest possible case for competent, personal spiritual direction as the most fundamental of all pastoral needs. Without such direction the Church's function cannot get off the ground. Yet nowhere is direction specifically mentioned. He speaks of the pastor's '. . . advising, counselling, teaching . . .' (p.181). He warns the pastor against becoming 'an educationalist, marriage guidance counsellor or a social worker . . .' (p.183). 'The problem is that there are few models for pastoral work which are now universally recognized by the laity . . . Thus the pastor role tends to drift . . .' Dare I suggest that spiritual direction might be the model that Reed, and the Church,

120

are looking for? Finally '. . . if laity find it hard to change roles from a W-activity dominated system to an S-activity dominated system, it justifies the need for tough training for clergy to enable them to do it, so that they can make it possible for others' (p.207).

I cannot refrain from pointing out how *The Dynamics of Religion* is so deeply similar to, if superficially different from, my *Pastoral Theology: a Reorientation*, published as long ago as 1956. The fundamental theses are the same, though expressed in very different idiom: neither can wholly avoid its own jargon. The points of meeting may be described thus:

(a) Functional as against dysfunctional religion means concentration on the oscillation process between extra- and intra-dependence through S-activity issuing in W-activity. To put it my way, creative religion is based on *regula*, which is a system whereby a series of conscious acts of prayer leads to habitual recollection, the basis of which is spiritual direction involving the application of ascetical theology.

(b) Reed speaks of the centrality of the 'worshipping group' (p.199, 212f.) which I prefer to call the Faithful Remnant. Both terms refer to a creative minority whose function is to glorify God in vicarious and practical service to the whole of society. We both aim at, in Reed's terms, communal rather than associational pastoral policy. We both wholeheartedly reject ecclesiasticism— pious self-centredness—folk-religion, and secularism. We both agree that 'The only church is the Body of Christ universal' (p.197). Here Reed appears to have some difficulty in seeing the relation between the parish, the diocese, and this Church universal, opposing narrow parochialism (ecclesiasticism) yet finally seeing the parish as the only socially operative unit (pp.191-200). May I draw attention to my own solution, which I think is St Paul's as well, and which sees parish and diocese as microcosmic of the whole Church Catholic? For it is this which makes final sense of the vicarious principle upon which we both rely so much, and which ultimately depends on the vicarious sacrifice of Jesus Christ himself.

(c) We both distrust head-counting, shallow recruitment which is not evangelism, or multitudinism to use my own atrocious bit of invented jargon. We both put Prayer in the centre of everything, but my Prayer, with an initial capital, includes anything from momentary acts of recollection to elaborate liturgy. In fact we are both aiming, I think, at the same ultimate; in his term functional, apostolic religion, and in my term Christian proficiency through *Regula*.

My friendly, and oblique criticism of *The Dynamics of Religion* underlines my reason for attempting this book: it so plainly advocates spiritual direction as our deepest need but without quite getting round to saying so. The term is nowhere mentioned, yet the underlying oscillation process is to be ensured, enabled, assisted, made possible. Regression to extra-dependence happens when opportunities are provided; it has to be assisted, there has to be teaching, counselling: anything but direction, yet that is what it all boils down to and that is clearly what is meant.

Having said that, it is fair to enumerate the positive contributions Reed makes to my own thesis here presented:

(a) Overall the very fact of the correspondence between the two approaches is enlightening. Support for orthodox direction based on traditional ascetic from so unlikely a source offers more than apologetic value. More specifically:

(b) Reed enlightens my directorial distinction between amateur and professional client as described in chapter 6, section 1. I distinguished between two spiritual types, two modes of *attrait*, but without judgement except in so far as personal preference supports the amateur. But personal preference and *attrait* should rigorously be curbed in direction; the skill is to guide those who are totally unlike oneself. Reed suggests that my preference may be objectively justified, or that amateur and professional indicate a two-stage progression rather than two types of equal value: the move from professional to amateur is an advance.

The professional in my sense is the man or woman who surrounds him or herself with all the paraphernalia of devotion; icons, images, holy pictures and so on. The amateur does without all that: a cabbage is as good as a crucifix. The former is extra-dependent upon the tangible symbol, which is fair enough, but he cannot regress to intra-dependence; he cannot easily get on without it, and he ought to be able to. On the other hand it is a little arrogant to assume that one is sufficiently intra-dependent—self resourceful—to get along without the traditional symbols all the time. It is the difference between medieval peasant-Catholicism and Puritanism, but Reed's interpretation, even his sociological terminology, clarifies the issue.

122

(c) The same terminology sorts out the problem of paternalism. Intra-dependence, as such, disclaims the need for direction altogether. Regression to extra-dependence acknowledges the need of help from a director, while further regression to intra-dependence is the proper end of a directorial interview. The right sort of paternalism is that which accepts the need for direction and which gives a sane authority to the director. The wrong kind is that which remains in this extra-dependent rut and one's director becomes indispensable. It is the personal aspect of the oscillation process. From the director's angle his job is to diagnose, classify, guide, coach, with unashamed paternalism, but only in order that his client can progress without him. The coach must coach the player, but it is the player who plays the game; no one can play his game for him, nobody can offer him second-by-second instruction while the game is in progress.

(d) S-activity, or concern with the symbols of the Church is a subtle concept. It means more than tangible or visible symbolism, extending to include creeds, prayers, liturgy and doctrinal formulae. The phrase might be translated as theology, but the sort which can be both taught and subconsciously absorbed. It means more than intellectualism; so the enabling of this activity, the bringing of it about, means spiritual direction. S-activity, the manifest function of the Church in prayer and liturgy, can only be absorbed by the client, not taught by the director. It points to applied theology, or ascetic, and goes a long way to show just how such application takes place: direction not teaching.

(e) The thesis illustrated by the diagram on p.170 of Reed's book offers valuable insights into the working of the vicarious principle. Experience and faith convince the Christian of the reality of the vicarious power of the worshipping faithful. Influence on society, conversion of individuals, occur when the divine office, the Holy Eucharist and positive guidance of the faithful take place as the Church's central activity. Now it is the sociologist's turn to ask, yes but how?—and why? And it is the sociologist himself who gives the answer. To say that priest, pastor, evangelist and prophet assist regression to extra-dependence through their various roles, and that society benefits from the interpretation of the Christian symbol (S-activity) leading to regression to intra-dependence (W-activity); to say all that sounds only like another, or the same, hypothesis in a different kind of language. But it says more than that; it goes some way to explain in sociological and psychological terms just how and why things do happen in this way.

In a striking passage on p.174, Reed demonstrates how in the modern Western world the whole concept of dependence is unpopular, which is only to say that the Pelagian heresy is still with us. Yet all are led to dependence upon something or someone; it is an existential experience, and therefore the right way to begin, in direction or evangelism, is to interpret Christian symbolism. If dependence is unfashionable, sin, repentance, spiritual discipline and humility are even more so; in fact they can be meaningless as an initial approach to modern people. All these deeper things will enter in but the concept of dependence is the contemporary springboard, more amenable to modern sophistication.

Chapter 15

Some Practical Guidelines

IF ALL CLIENTS are unique then so are their spiritual directors. I have tried to keep my arguments reasonably factual and objective, attempting—with whatever little success—to exert some discipline over my personal viewpoint. If I am still a little unhappy about 'ministerial skills' I am even more so with pastoralia presented in the context of autobiography, however venerable the author might be. Nevertheless there are certain personal views which might be worth minimal consideration; if only in so far as they spell out certain points already made.

1. *The relationship*

I have claimed the director-client relationship to be unique. This does not mean that we can learn nothing from the study of personal relationships as given by psychologist and sociologist, but it does mean that we must take their teaching with critical humility. In all such person-to-person interviews the first rule is to listen rather than talk; we have to heed the common warnings that in all professional spheres the client is apt to expect too much. The doctor's patient wants an instant cure, the solicitor's client a cut-and-dried solution. But direction is a longer, continuous process, and over-expectancy is likely to creep in later rather than sooner. By this time the relationship should have become established and here I must diverge from the counsellor.

It is at this point that psychiatrist and counsellor warn of the intrusion of an emotional element. Clients become attached to those upon whom they become—to return to Reed—extra-dependent. The emotional relation happens in direction as well, but instead of the warning I think this is to be accepted, even welcomed. Many directors will disagree in horror, but St Teresa, St

François de Sales, St Aelred, perhaps St Paul, certainly St John, and hosts of others seem to be on my side. Over-expectation, the wrong sort of paternalism, is alleviated by the deepening of a relationship that becomes a mutual quest rather than an authoritarian discipline: the director–client relation must never become a battle of wits.

I prefer to speak of those under my direction as clients for reasons already given, but director–client eventually becomes father–child and finally brother–brother. All three analogies outlined in chapter 4 are still needed. It is the psychiatrist and counsellor who more easily talk of clients, but do not they really mean patients? For in these contexts the emotional aspect is dangerous and the battle of wits inevitable. I am not thinking of the schoolgirl's crush on the handsome curate nor of the merry widow with clerical inclinations, but of that deeper relation between two whole people which inevitably grows out of love-on-the-slab. It is the love of Christ shared equally. And if, because of human frailty an element of emotional risk arises then I believe that that risk has to be taken.

2. *The setting*

All face-to-face professionalism gives considerable thought to the setting for the interview; should one sit pompously behind a huge desk with the client perched upright on a hard chair, or should armchairs be provided for both? There is obviously much significance in the psychiatrist's couch. The directorial problem is a little different.

It is obvious that spiritual direction spells two armchairs and no desk, and no couch! The cold slab is metaphorical. But where? In pastoral circles there are three answers: in the first place it is argued that hospitality is a Christian virtue biblically exhorted, so one's own Christian home, one's own friendly fireside is the natural place for this sort of pastoral care. There is something to be said for it, and I think a little more to be said against it. By way of preface I noted with interest and considerable agreement the sociologist's conclusion that modern people prefer, and pro-fessionally trust, the doctor's clinic, the supermarket, the lawyer's office, and the place where professional people work, which is not at home.

As the relation develops from director–client to brothers-in-Christ, hospitality may well come in; no personal friends are debarred from the homes of doctors, lawyers, or managers of supermarkets, while it remains doubtful if these friendly homes are the right places for business.

Secondly, old-fashioned bishops plumped for the church as the proper setting for pastoral guidance, mainly I suspect because it was a little more respectable where lady clients were concerned. I am all in favour of extending the use of churches beyond liturgical activity, but again there are snags. Remote country churches can, regrettably, be dank, cold and lonely, with little protection against the designing amazon: barely congenial for a tête-à-tête of any sort. On the other hand large city churches and cathedrals bustle with all sorts of activity, especially in the tourist season. The old-fashioned bishops would be happy with the chaperone element, apart from which it is not so good.

I used to be unhappy with the American-style parish complex: church, office, coffee room, club and so on. It seemed to be putting the emphasis in the wrong place. I was also unhappy about group-team ministries worked from a central office, surgery, clinic or whatever. Perhaps I have been unwittingly influenced by those sociological factors already alluded to; I have certainly changed my mind, for this is the third choice and I think the best one.

The director's room, study, office, within the church complex or precinct but away from his home, offers all the advantages. But its furnishings and arrangements are significant and offer scope for personal imagination. To my mind the place should look cosily efficient but not too blatantly clinical. It should contain one's working library, reference to which is frequently demanded if direction is to be competent. There have to be files, office equipment and a nice big desk—but not to peer at one's client over—well out of the way of a couple of comfortable chairs. Then a very carefully selected group of pictures and ornaments: holy ones to please the 'professional' client and some secular ones to put the 'amateur' at ease. Not quite the clinical surgery but not quite the domestic hearth either.

Casual observation suggests that doctors are rather bad at this, and dentists, especially those who deal with children, are very good at it. In any setting a dental chair is a formidable object, but it loses much of its terror when surrounded by pictures, cartoons, tropical fish and quiet background pop.

3. *The confessional*

I have deliberately said little about the part played by the sacrament of penance in spiritual direction. This is in reaction to the common mistake of assuming that confession and direction are one and the same thing, or that confessional counsel is the main vehicle for direction. As a good Anglican I also uphold the view that competent direction is possible without the sacrament of penance at all, and as a good Catholic that a client's director and confessor need not necessarily be the same person. This is an important principle when proficient direction by qualified laity is healthily on the increase.

Nevertheless the sacrament of penance is to be encouraged: it helps, and in various ways. It helps the director to discern the intricacies of *attrait*, and especially in so far as basically healthy aspects of it may nevertheless need to be disciplined. It helps the client for the obvious reason that sin is the greatest enemy of prayer, and its eradication the most positive preparation for progress. In the context of direction how ought it best to be administered?

The traditional method, brief, objective, factual, is well enough known, but it has recently come under criticism for risking formalism, superstition and mechanical unreality. So experiments have been made to loosen the structure by substituting the confessional box for a little confessional room (back to the two armchairs) where personal sin can be discussed and confessed less formally. The final method follows the fashion towards group-corporate expression in which personal and private confession are set in a liturgical context.

The possible errors associated with the first method are more likely to arise when the sacrament is divorced from direction and regarded as a private and subjective incidental. Direction itself guards against such distortion, and within it this traditional method remains probably the best.

The second method is defensible, especially as a method of guidance in preparation, and for the benefit of a particular temperament. But it is apt to confuse confession with the total directorial process. The third, liturgical or group method may well have a general pastoral value but it could be accused of following the group-fashion. Since direction is essentially a face-to-face, one-to-one affair the first and traditional way is to be preferred.

4. *Some practical guidelines*

Learning comes before everything, including holiness and experience, and I believe that if the theological schema of this book is adhered to, creative direction will follow. But this is not to deny the value of experience, even my own; we do not start from scratch with each new client—although scratch remains the best of starting points—yet certain attitudes and errors, images and analogies, crop up so frequently that these might be discussed as secondary sources of some value.

(a) *Baptismal incorporation and the nuptial analogy.* Both have been previously treated in the theological sections of this book, and both go together since baptism is, as it were, our marriage to Christ, hence the analogy of husband–wife and God–man in a similar relationship. The analogy may be stretched to its limits and there is hardly an aspect of the spiritual life that cannot be illuminated by it. It invariably crops up in the initial interview if only because, asked what is the absolute foundation of Christian prayer, only the smallest minority of clients give baptism as the answer. Once prayer is interpreted as a continuous and given relation with God in Christ a host of minor yet common difficulties vanish: 'Dearest, we have had a lovely evening together but I am afraid my mind wandered once or twice . . .' 'It is wonderful being with you dear, but I do not seem to be making much progress . . .' The analogy puts this sort of nonsense firmly in its place.

(b) *Rule-breaking and poor prayer.* There are seven capital sins and nobody has ever managed to invent an eighth, although the faithful continue to try. One of the seven is spiritual sloth, which might lead to failure properly to embrace *regula*, but there is no sin called rule-breaking. So with 'praying badly', or with periodic aridity. The *askesis* analogy helps here, because the spiritual athlete can be out of form, he can go through a bad patch when nothing goes right, or he can simply perform badly and lose. None of this is sin, and yet so many clients think that it is. Cheating, dishonesty, the deliberate foul; these are sins. Playing badly is not.

(c) *Progress.* Life in Christ is a marriage, not a courtship. Both may be said to progress, but the basis of marriage is stability, with progress as a long-term development, imperceptibly subtle. If it is to be assessed at all it must be in terms of years rather than weeks, hence the warnings against misinterpretation of the classic scales, ladders and journeys. Prayer, like marriage, is to be lived out daily, without constant re-appraisal as to how things are working out. Spiritual progress is important but it is too often misinterpreted.

(d) *The corporate and vicarious aspect.* In spite of the prevailing fashion which puts all the emphasis on the community and the group, a one-sided individualism remains a constant Anglican temptation. It is still difficult to convince a congregation that it is a team and not an audience. In spiritual direction the majority of clients need the constant reminder of their vicarious efficacy, however well this doctrine is intellectually understood and accepted.

Satisfying and demanding intercession, centred on the Eucharist, is obviously directed at others, while the embrace of *regula* in its entirety is the supreme redemptive vehicle. But when difficulties arise, when things go wrong, the emphasis is liable to switch to the personal: there is aridity, dullness, weakness and frailty, and *I* feel awful. The point missed, which any proficient Christian knows well enough in theory, is that such personal feelings are of little importance, and that, however distressing to the client concerned, the vicarious efficacy of *regula* is unimpaired. The ambulance syndrome insinuates itself into prayer; the spiritual director is looked upon as one who cures faults rather than as one who develops gifts.

Recognition of this element is usually of support to the client because his outgoing spiritual work for others outweighs his personal pain. A police officer fulfils his service to the community by being a police officer and doing his duty as efficiently as possible. There must be occasions when he enjoys the job and occasions when it is most unpleasant; he has jobs which are exciting and those which are boring. But the society which he serves does not, and should not, consider his inner feelings, which have little to do with the service he gives. Prayer follows a similar pattern through the vicarious principle.

(e) *Grace and nature.* St Thomas Aquinas taught that grace perfects nature and does not destroy it. This sublime doctrine offers the widest pastoral-theological implications, but with a special, narrower concern for spiritual direction. For various reasons, woolliness of direction and misdirected spiritual reading amongst them, clients are for ever apologizing for being what they are, while having an oblique grumble at God for not having made them somebody else. At bottom it is the capital sin of envy masquerading as humility. What so often happens is that a client worries, grumbles and bemoans the fact that he cannot make imaginative meditations, or he finds difficulty with intercession, or he cannot understand simple contemplation; he is too fond of the good things of this life and finds theology desperately boring. Oh dear, what can he do about it?

There can be no hard and fast rules, but the frequent answer is nothing; do not try to do anything about it because he is not supposed to be this kind of Christian anyway. His gifts may lie in a different direction, but the wrong books, and perhaps the wrong retreat conductor, have conned him into believing that he really ought to be somebody else: why does not grace destroy his nature?

Heaven forfend an Anglican index of prohibited books, or directorial restriction on his client's freedom of choice, but it should be responsible choice. There are times and occasions when teaching which goes against the grain of *attrait* fulfils a useful purpose, but we must realize what we are doing. Those in any way concerned with the guidance of others must read as widely as possible, trying to understand approaches at variance with their own, but again they must know what they are doing. The tenor in the choir should understand the bass part, but he should not try to sing it. Hence the importance of the slab for ascertaining precisely what the client is, how God has chosen to put him together.

(f) *Fellowship.* Psychiatrists and clinical psychologists advocate the introduction of clients to similar-minded people, or those with the same sort of problem. In direction such introduction should be unnecessary since the local Christian community should supply the need. But fellowship is an ambiguous word with various strata of meaning. The biblical word—*koinonia*—indicates its deepest meaning: fellowship in the Lord, fellowship in the Gospel, and this should be nurtured. It is regrettable that, lacking New Testament spontaneity, it often has to be, but it is a valuable ancillary and support to direction. Clients should be encouraged to discuss their pilgrimage of prayer, to talk about it, thus entering into a solid partnership in Christ. It has to be encouraged because of English reticence about such things, even amongst the faithful, and because of the evil type of comprehensiveness which dictates that nobody may be more enthusiastic than anyone else: the unholy mediocrity. It is a pity that such should be: one does not have to give artificial stimulus to golfers to talk about golf, or anglers to discuss fishing—the task here is to restrain them—but prayer is still a taboo subject.

Such oils the wheels of direction and points to the final synthesis: spiritual direction is the most burdensome responsibility, and the most joyous game. It is *koinonia* in the Lord.

Appendices

THERE IS controversy as to whether theological discussion may properly be supplemented graphically; by plans, diagrams, graphs and so on. Fifty years ago such an expedient would have been frowned upon most severely; if a theological thesis could not be clearly stated in words then it was unlikely that it could be explained in any other way.

Twenty-five years ago I remember an internationally acclaimed bishop and professor making the same point, but followed—just for fun—by a plan of God's creative relation to the universe drawn in multi-coloured chalk on a gigantic blackboard. I found some of his arguments a little obscure, but I can still reproduce the plan in detail. It is a matter of taste, of a liking for or dislike of visual symbolism, of a mind which is intellectually clear or imaginatively stimulated.

The tide has turned full circle, for today visual aids, as they are called, are part of the general educational scene. And indeed beyond it, for in an age of international tourism and the European Economic Community, even 'Ladies' and 'Gentlemen' are publicly displayed in symbols.

The following appendices are offered as such a matter of taste; I hope that they will clarify certain issues for some readers, knowing full well that they might confuse others and infuriate some more. But following the late Bishop Ian Ramsey (for he it was to whom I referred), it is just for fun: not to be taken too seriously.

A further difficulty arises with the complexity of the subject matter involved. Over the years, and for various reasons and occasions, I have attempted the plan of the development and inter-relations of the Western schools of prayer (Appendix I). The overall pattern remains fairly constant but the details come out differently each time. Were I to ask half a dozen colleagues to attempt the same diagram the result could be the same: a common outline with differences in detail. When I published my study of *English Spirituality* I was assailed by several friends and brothers for claiming that the Franciscan School was only a minor influence in this development. As objective ascetical theology (or as objective as it can be) I still think I was right, but the debate continues and is unlikely to be resolved. So play with my plan if it amuses, otherwise disregard it.

Appendix II is even more prone to personal interpretation, however disciplined one tries to be. It will be noted, for example, that both St Anselm and Julian of Norwich occupy the same position within the speculative and affective balance. At first sight the two look very different, yet on deeper study it is discovered that St Anselm the disciplined philosopher was also a saint of profound devotion. Julian of Norwich—the vividly emotional (some would say hysterical) feminine mystic—was also a very profound theologian. It depends on how you look and what you seek. A typical English cottage garden has neat rows of vegetables in the middle, interspersed with a few standard roses, delphiniums, lupins and foxgloves on the perimeter. One would call it a vegetable garden with some flowers around it; another would say that it was a flower garden with vegetables in the middle. It is like A. N. Whitehead's bifurcation theory; in plain language you see what you are looking for. St Anselm and Julian are rather like the cottage garden. But the debate continues.

In such spirit I offer the following appendices, hopefully for enlightenment, certainly for fun.

Appendices

Appendix I

The ascetical syllabus, or the tools of the trade for spiritual direction, as outlined in chapter 7, and further elaborated in chapters 8-11.

THE ASCETICAL-THEOLOGICAL SOURCES

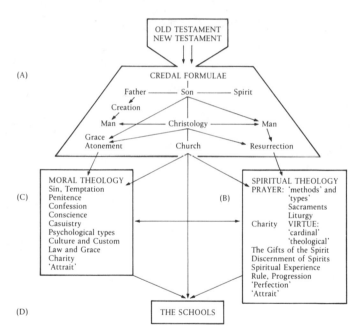

(D) THE SCHOOLS: Key to diagram opposite

The following diagram attempts to illustrate the development of Christian Spirituality through the centuries. The first four centuries form part of the essential theological background for a study of the Schools (i.e. from (A), (B), (C), to (D) see pp. 48-53.)

1 The fourteen most fundamental and significant Schools are in bold caps, e.g. **BENEDICTINE**. They are followed by the most significant writers of that School.

2 Proper names in caps, e.g. BASIL, are writers whose basic theology is especially significant to ascetical theology, and which has given rise to a particular School, e.g. Augustine—Austin Canons Regular—Victorine School; Aquinas—Dominican School.

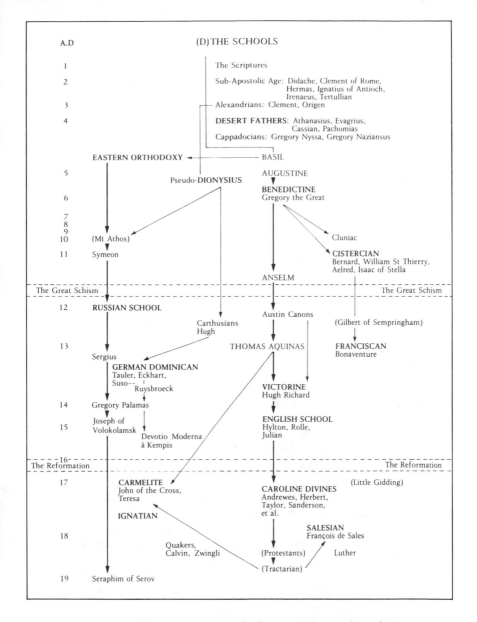

3 Lower case indicates important schools or movements but of lesser significance to the student of Spiritual Direction, e.g. Quakers.

4 Bracketed lower case indicate important historical developments, illustrative of original spiritual thrusts, but which have left little or no ascetical theology in writing, e.g. (Gilbert of Sempringham).

The overall purpose here is to try to produce a logical scheme of study over five, ten, fifteen years; to provide a basic background plan in outline, which may be filled in as students advance. Absolutely no judgemental inference is implied as to the intrinsic value of a School or writer. There are purposeful omissions for the sake of clarity. A plan containing hundreds more entries, spread over a couple of square yards, could be produced. I do not think that it would help!

Appendix II

The Speculative-Affective Synthesis. Although *attrait* is always to be nurtured, with certain curbs and restraints as part of that nurture, a sane balance between the speculative and affective remains an ideal. Such a synthesis forms the central core, the 'major key', of Anglican spirituality, and is expressed by the classic phrase 'true piety and sound learning'.

The following diagram, confined to the Western tradition, is offered with all the reservations already expressed, and hopefully as a framework for further thought and study rather than simplification. Whatever else, it could certainly form the basis for debate, discussion and argument.

It is unrealistic to talk about 'schools of prayer' during the first millennium of the Christian era, since from the Western and pastoral viewpoint Benedictinism reigned supreme and alone. Yet these thousand years demand serious study since they contain the seeds of all that was to come. Three introductory points might be noted:

1. The Bible remains at the root of everything, containing all future elements in embryo. It contains all doctrine, yet its idiom is the God-man relation spelled out in experiential rather than intellectual terms. The Bible contains all doctrine, and clearly states a good deal of theology, but it is not primarily a doctrinal treatise. So in ascetical terms it comes just on the affective side. It might be suggested, moreover, that despite St Paul and St John, the Old Testament is slightly more speculative than the New Testament, since it is concerned with the *Covenant* relation: man's duty to God in terms of obedience to his commandments, social, liturgical and moral. The New Testament concerns *encounter* and *incorporation*, with and in Christ, which implies a strong affective element.

138

2. The sub-Apostolic age was still influenced by *parousia*: Christ was soon to return, while his known presence was plain and obvious to all. There was no need for elaborate schemes of meditation and contemplative prayer, nor for much theology except for a firm conviction and experience of the Resurrection. The period has much to give to the spiritual director in this present century, but it must come outside most of the categories.

3. Devotion in the first millennium was expressed largely by liturgy as expression of a developing theology; there were no 'methods' of personal prayer. This whole vast period, therefore, tends towards the speculative side. There are exceptions, or outcrops of affectiveness, within the Benedictine tradition, and in the Egyptian Desert.

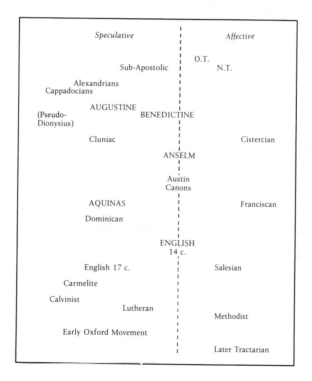

Index